W9-BEM-561

A Kid's Guide To Washington, D.C.

Copyright © 1989 by Harcourt Brace & Company

All rights reserved. No part of this publication may be
reproduced or transmitted in any form or by any means,
electronic or mechanical, including photocopy,
recording, or any information storage and retrieval
system, without permission in writing from
the publisher.

Requests for permission to make copies of any part of the
work should be mailed to: Permissions Department,
Harcourt Brace & Company, 6277 Sea Harbor Drive,
Orlando, Florida 32887-6777.

Written by Diane C. Clark
Illustrations and maps by Richard E. Brown
Designed by G. B. D. Smith

Gulliver Books is a registered trademark of
Harcourt Brace & Company.

Library of Congress Cataloging-in-Publication Data
Clark, Diane C.
A kid's guide to Washington, D.C./[written by Diane C.
Clark; illustrations and maps by Richard E. Brown]—
1st ed.
vi, 153 p.   : ill., maps: 24 cm. (Gulliver travels)
"Gulliver Books."
Summary: Presents a travel guide to Washington, D.C.,
featuring games, puzzles, and other activities.
ISBN 0-15-200459-9
1. Washington (D.C.)—Guidebooks—Juvenile literature.
2. Children—Travel—Washington (D.C.)—
Guidebooks—Juvenile literature. I. Brown, Richard E., ill.
II. Title. III. Series
F192.3.C53   1989
917.53′044—dc20   89-127208

Printed in the United States of America

S R Q P O N M

C·O·N·T·E·N·T·S

How to Use This Book

Are you about to visit Washington, D.C.? Read this book before you leave, then carry it with you while you're there. It will help you choose where you want to go each day.

But don't just read it! Write in this book. Color some of the pictures. Keep track of your trip in the travel diary. Use the maps: try to figure out where you are and where you want to go. There are games and puzzles all through the book for you to do while riding in a car or plane, waiting to eat, or just hanging around waiting for the grown-ups to get going!

The first part of the book tells you what the weather is like in Washington (so you'll know what kind of clothes to bring), the different ways you can travel into the city, and how to get around once you're there.

T·R·A·V·E·L D·I·A·R·Y

My name is _____.

I live at _____.

in _____.

My phone number is (____) ____ – _____

I'm taking a trip to _____

from _____. I'm traveling with

_____, and we plan to be away from home for

____ days. My parents' full names are _____

_____ and _____.

In case of an emergency, they can be reached at (____)

____ – _____ or you can call _____

_____ at (____)

_____

____ – _____.

❖ ❖ ❖

my picture

Birthday _____

Age _____

Sex _____

Height _____

Weight _____

Eye color _____

Hair color _____

Following this introduction are chapters about the history, government, people, and animals that have made Washington, D.C., such a popular vacation spot. There are also descriptions of places to visit and tips on where to eat and where to get the most unusual souvenirs.

The calendar of events will let you know what special annual activities are going on while you're in Washington, D.C.—such as parades, festivals, and ceremonies.

If you need particular information about a place you want to visit, like the time it opens, the address, or the phone number, you can find it in the appendix. Following the appendix, you'll discover a number of

Welcome to Washington, D.C.

Can you locate Washington, D.C., on a map? It's that
little spot on the East Coast bordered by Maryland on
the north and Virginia on the south.

It doesn't look like much, does it? After all, compare it with the size of California or Texas. Washington even makes tiny Rhode Island look huge. Yet this 69-square-mile area is the capital of the country, the headquarters of the government, and the home of embassies representing countries all over the world.

Every year Washington is visited by royalty, government heads, business leaders, and 19 million tourists just like you.

A trip to Washington, D.C., has lots of surprises and adventures in store—things that you can't see or do anywhere else in the world. For one, you'll get to witness government in action and see how bills are passed on issues such as setting the highway speed limit or the amount of taxes your parents pay. You may even meet your own senator.

Did you know?

More than 130 countries have embassies in Washington. You can spot them because the flag of the country flies out front.

You'll find out where the president and first lady live. And you'll see the highest court in the nation and the largest library in the world.

If you're a fan of James Bond, you'll enjoy the FBI's real-life spying devices and true stories about tracking criminals from such small clues as a smidgen of paint the size of a pin prick.

And money—you'll see more money than Uncle Scrooge could hoard in a lifetime when you visit the printing plant that manufactures all of our country's dollar bills.

Did you know?

July 4, 1776, is known as the date of the signing of the Declaration of Independence. This isn't quite true. It was adopted on July 4, but it wasn't actually signed until August 2, 1776.

You'll also get a chance to step back in history. You can visit places where time stands still; places where "colonial" families and farmers till soil and churn butter just like they did 300 years ago. You can even eat gingerbread made from the recipe of George Washington's mother, Mary Washington. You'll see a replica of George Washington's teeth and resolve the mystery question, Were they really made out of wood?

You can also see the Declaration of Independence, the gun that killed Abraham Lincoln, a fence made from Civil War muskets, cannonballs still lodged in houses, and the church pew where Civil War general Robert E. Lee sat.

And that's just the beginning. There are many other thrilling sights: the ruby slippers worn by Dorothy in *The Wizard of Oz,* and the flag that inspired the "Star Spangled Banner." Or, how about the largest blue diamond in the world, a real dinosaur egg, or an eighteenth-century man whose body turned to soap?

Want to see the *Kitty Hawk,* the plane that flew Orville and Wilbur Wright into the history books? Or walk through *Skylab?* Or touch a piece of moon rock? You can do all these things and more on your trip, if time allows.

But first, let's learn a little bit more about Washington, D.C.

T·R·A·V·E·L D·I·A·R·Y

Of all the places I've heard about in Washington, D.C., I'm most excited about seeing _____.

because _____

Other things I want to see are _____

_____

❖ ❖ ❖

Whom do you think Washington was named for? If you said *George Washington*, our country's first president, you were right.

But do you know what *D.C.* stands for? It means *District of Columbia.* You see, Washington, D.C., is not a state. And unlike you, people who live in Washington, D.C., do not have legislators who can vote for them in Congress. They have one delegate who can speak out on their behalf, but he can only vote in smaller committee meetings.

For many years the people who lived in Washington, D.C., weren't even allowed to vote for president. But in 1964 that changed and now they can.

Did you know?

Washington, D.C., was not always the name of our capital. It was originally called *Federal City.*

Test yourself

Q: What city was the first temporary capital of the United States?

A: Philadelphia.

PACKING FOR THE TRIP

What you bring to Washington, D.C., depends on the season. In winter it doesn't snow very often, but the weather is cold and rainy. You'll need warm pants, sweaters, a coat, mittens, a scarf, and a hat. Since snow quickly turns to slush, waterproof boots and comfortable shoes for sightseeing are a must.

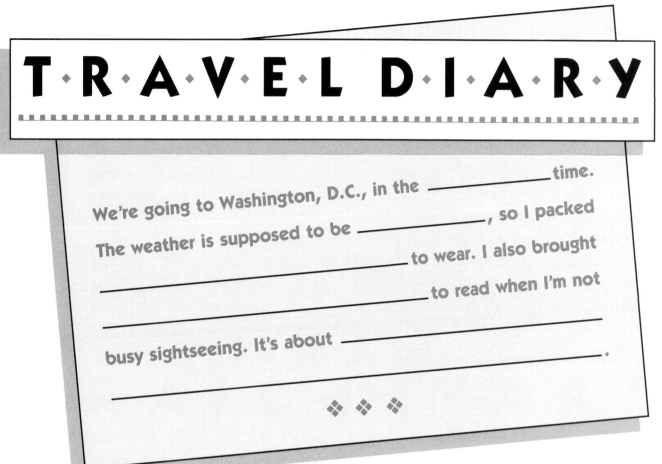

T·R·A·V·E·L D·I·A·R·Y

We're going to Washington, D.C., in the _____ time.

The weather is supposed to be _____, so I packed

_____ to wear. I also brought

_____ to read when I'm not

busy sightseeing. It's about _____

_____

❖ ❖ ❖

Did you know?

In 1912, the city of Tokyo, Japan, gave 3,000 cherry trees to the U.S. That's where Washington's cherry blossoms come from.

Washington's spring lives up to the saying, "April showers bring May flowers." Be sure to take your umbrella and raincoat. Even if it sprinkles, Washington is at its most beautiful in spring, with the cherry trees, forsythia, and azaleas in full bloom.

Summers are hot and muggy with temperatures in the 90's. It's T-shirt-and-shorts time. Fall is crisp and cool. Bring some warm clothes—and yes, an umbrella. Washington often gets autumn showers, too.

GETTING THERE

It's easy to get to Washington, D.C. You can come by car, bus, train, plane, or even boat.

Flying is very popular. More than 22 million people fly into one of the area's 3 airports each year. The closest is Washington National Airport, just 15 minutes from the White House and across the Potomac River, which separates Washington from Virginia. Try to grab a window seat, because as you land, you'll get a great view of the Capitol, the Washington Monument, and the Lincoln and Jefferson Memorials.

T·R·A·V·E·L D·I·A·R·Y

We will be traveling by _____ to get to Washington, D.C. We'll be leaving from _____ and arriving in _____ to begin our trip. We will travel through _____ on our way to Washington. I am ____ hours/ ____ days/ ____ miles away from home. Once we get to Washington, D.C., we will be staying at _____.

Washington Dulles International Airport, also in Virginia, is about 45 minutes from downtown Washington, D.C. You'll fly in over trees and fields, but imagine what this area might have looked like in 1862. In August and September of that year, the land surrounding Dulles was a battleground in the second Bull Run clash of the Civil War.

The third airport is the Baltimore-Washington International Airport, about 50 minutes north of the city, in Maryland.

Driving into Washington—whether you come from the north, south, or west—takes you past historic towns and battle sites.

If you're arriving from Richmond, Virginia, you'll pass close by the Pamunkey Indian Reservation. Remember that the first North American Indians to meet European settlers were the Indians of Virginia and Maryland. The Pamunkeys planted crops here 10,000 years before the birth of Christ. There is now a museum and a reconstructed sixteenth-century village on the reservation. At nearby Mattaponi Indian Reservation, you can see Pocahontas's necklace, Chief Opecanough's tomahawk, and listen to Indian princess Minnie Ha-Ha Custalow tell the legends of her tribal ancestors.

Whether by car, train, bus, or plane, there was a route you had to follow to reach Washington, D.C. Color in the state where you live and draw a line tracing your path from home to Washington on the map on page 4.

Did you know?

Colonial explorer Captain John Smith first sailed up the Potomac River where Washington is now located in 1608.

You'll also pass by Jamestown, where Captain John Smith landed in 1607 and founded the first English colony in the New World. Nearby is Yorktown, where the revolutionary war was won.

Driving south from Baltimore, Maryland, brings you through former Indian territory, too. Several miles to the east is Chesapeake Bay—an arm of water jutting in from the Atlantic Ocean. Although much of the sea life has been depleted by pollution, many fishermen still make their living gathering the clams, oysters, and crabs for which Maryland is famous.

Just before entering Washington on the Baltimore-Washington Parkway, you'll pass the NASA Goddard Space Flight Center. Here you'll find an amazing collection of rockets and satellites. You can stop to see a model rocket launch the first and third Sundays of every month.

If you're arriving from the west, you could make a stop at Luray Caverns on U.S. Route 211. Stroll through cave after cave to view unusual rock formations. Some resemble fried eggs sunny-side up, strips of bacon, and Turkish towels like those hanging in your bathroom. These caverns, tunneling 164 feet underground, are the largest in the eastern United States.

If your family decides to ride the train into Washington, you'll arrive at Union Station, a grand old building completed in 1907. It's so big that you can easily get lost in its waiting room, so stay together.

GETTING AROUND

Finding your way around many cities is a nightmare, but Washington, D.C., was designed to be a snap. Think of it as a rectangle, with the Capitol anchored at lower center like the hub of a wheel. Four spokes come out from the Capitol at right angles, dividing the city into 4 sections. The spokes are North Capitol Street, South Capitol Street, East Capitol Street and, on the west side of the building, instead of an actual street, the grassy Mall. The 4 sections of Washington are called *Northwest (NW)*, *Northeast (NE)*, *Southwest (SW)*, and *Southeast (SE)*. You can always tell what section of the city you're in by looking at a street sign—all street names are followed by one of these abbreviations.

WASHINGTON, D.C.

Within each of these 4 areas the roads running north and south are numbered—1st Street, 2nd Street, 3rd Street, and so on. The roads running east and west are named after letters of the alphabet—C Street, D Street, E Street, and so forth. There are no A or B Streets because A Street became the Mall and East Capitol Street, and B Street was renamed Constitution Avenue on the north side of the Mall and Independence Avenue on the south side.

After the letters are used up, street names become words in alphabetical order. This alphabetical lineup keeps repeating itself until it reaches the Maryland and Virginia borders.

A few major avenues run diagonally across the district and are named after states such as Massachusetts, Connecticut, and Pennsylvania.

Did you know?

The letter *J* was left out when Washington streets were named. To this day, no one knows why.

Here's a problem for you to solve on your own: If you are at Third and Constitution, NW, and want to go to Third and F Street, NW, how many blocks will you have to travel? (You can use the map on page 16 to figure this out.)

(Answer on page 145)

Knowing the layout of the city makes it easy to figure out where you are and how to get where you're going. For instance, if you are at 14th and E Streets, NW, and need to go to the Capitol, you have to walk 14 blocks to the east and 4 blocks to the south. If you are at 16th and M Streets and need to get to 12th and K Streets, you go 2 blocks down to K Street and 4 blocks over to 12th Street.

It's amazing to think that this simple street plot was designed about 200 years ago by Washington's first city planner, Frenchman Pierre L'Enfant. But it's not a perfect grid because L'Enfant's design wasn't completed until long after his death and more streets had to be added as the city grew.

Even though streets are easy to locate, your parents may not want to drive in Washington because parking is hard to find and very expensive. The best way to get around is by taxi, bus, or subway.

Taxi fares are reasonable. A map of the zones is in the back of each cab. Every time you pass from one zone to another, the fare rises. It also increases at rush hour, during stormy weather, and if there are extra people in the cab.

Did you know?

Pierre L'Enfant, whose clever Washington, D.C., street plan is praised today, died in poverty in 1825.

You can go almost anywhere in Washington by bus. If you want to check the schedule and figure out what buses to take, call Metrobus. Even if you don't call, bus drivers are friendly and can point you in the right direction.

The Tourmobile is a special bus that runs continuously around the Mall and into Virginia, stopping at the top sight-seeing attractions along the way. If this is your first visit to Washington, D.C., you should invest in an all-day ticket, which allows you to get on and off the Tourmobile as often as you like.

More popular than the bus is the Metrorail. This subway system opened in 1976 and is one of the fastest and easiest ways to get around. You can find out how much it will cost to ride from one station to another by looking at the map near the ticket machines. Insert your money and your ticket will come out. Using the Metrorail can be confusing at first. If you have any questions, ask one of the attendants in the glass booth nearby.

Subway lines have different colors—blue, red, yellow, and orange. To catch your train, follow the sign and color announcing the final destination of the line you want to take. Be sure to check the front and sides of the train to make certain it's the right color, because sometimes 2 lines stop at the same place.

T·R·A·V·E·L D·I·A·R·Y

I rode the _____ subway to _____

_____. When we rode on

to see _____.

the subway, I _____.

The people on the subway were _____

I think subways are _____. If I was going to design a

subway, I would _____.

❖ ❖ ❖

If you head in the wrong direction, don't panic. Just get off at the next stop and hop on a train coming back the other way. Trains run from 5:30 A.M. to midnight, and there's usually no more than a 15-minute wait.

Now you're all set to find your way around the city. But first you need to know a little more about this unusual area and how it came to be.

A Brief History

WAY BACK WHEN

When European explorers first came to what is now Washington, D.C., they were met by native American Indians who lived in small villages scattered along the rivers and in the forests. The Europeans traded with the Indians, who taught them a lot about how to live in this strange "new" land. The settlers learned how to fish, and, more importantly, how to grow and use corn—one of the main foods of the Indians.

With the arrival of the European settlers who set up their own villages in this area came diseases unknown to the local Indians. Many died from these foreign illnesses and others moved away. By the 1600s there were almost no Indians left here.

COLONIAL AMERICA

In colonial times boys wore dresses and petticoats until age 4 or 5. Then they switched to adult-style clothes.

■ ■ ■

Women almost always wore a hat—even in the house. Men usually shaved off their hair and wore a powdered wig.

The settlers divided the land into farms, both large and small. Because there were no cities, the really big farms became centers of activity. These large farms were called *plantations*, and the rich landowners brought in slaves from Africa to work in their fields. The plantation owners lived comfortably, but small farmers, craftsmen, laborers, servants, and slaves had to work hard and long hours to survive.

Life in colonial America was far different than it is today. There was no electricity or plumbing. Many homes didn't even have kitchens. Cooking often was done in a separate building because of the danger of fire. The colonists ate simple food, and corn became a major part of their diet. They also hunted and ate rabbit, deer, squirrel, and pigeon. Because there was little milk, kids had to drink hard cider, beer, and wine—even for breakfast!

T·R·A·V·E·L D·I·A·R·Y

If I could go back in time to colonial America, I would want to be alive in the year _____. I would be a _____ and _____ for a living. I would live in a _____ made of _____. It would have ____ rooms and look like _____ _____.

❖ ❖ ❖

Very few children went to school back then. If a family was rich, it paid a teacher to live in the house and teach the kids there. Sometimes several farm families got together, built a small schoolhouse, and hired a teacher. Boys went to school longer than girls because girls were expected to get married at 16 or 17, raise a family, and keep house.

Because coins were scarce, the colonists often used tobacco leaves that they grew on their farms for money. They paid the doctor or bought a new wagon with tobacco. They even paid their taxes with tobacco.

Did you know?

Only the rich had dishes and silverware, so most people ate with their fingers.

■ ■ ■

There were no blackboards or pencils in colonial days. Students wrote with a lump of lead or with a goose-quill pen dipped in homemade ink. Paper was very expensive, so birch bark was used instead.

REVOLUTIONARY TIMES

The colonists, under the rule of England, became angry at having to pay taxes to a government clear across the Atlantic Ocean. They started to protest against British rule. That was the beginning of the American Revolution. In 1776, the 13 colonies declared their independence from England, and the United States was born.

Realizing that they needed a new government to take the place of the old, a group of men got together and wrote the Constitution, one of our nation's most important documents. In it they set down a framework for our country's government that we still use today. They chose George Washington, the general who led the colonists in the American Revolution, as their first president.

After the war, the lawmakers who wrote the Constitution met in various cities, but they decided this new country needed a permanent home for its government. President George Washington selected a site along the Potomac River that was partly in Maryland and partly in Virginia. And in 1790, the District of Columbia came into being.

Construction of the new city began. French-born engineer Pierre L'Enfant agreed to design Federal City (as Washington, D.C., was originally called). He chose a hill overlooking the area as the site of the Capitol Building. His plans were to create a magnificent city that would make the American people proud. L'Enfant's design was very grand, but his temper got in the way and he was fired.

A design was needed for the Capitol Building, and so a nationwide competition was held. The winning design was by William Thornton, a young doctor, and in 1793 George Washington laid the cornerstone of the Capitol Building. Work on the White House also was begun.

Did you know?

The North and South bickered over which would be the site of the nation's new capital. But the North gave up its claim when the new government agreed to pay the North's heavy revolutionary war debts. That's why today Washington, D.C., is on what was once Southern land.

■ ■ ■

When Congress arrived at its new capital in 1800, the site was not impressive. Cattle grazed on what is now the Mall, pigs roamed the streets, and snakes and mosquitoes were everywhere.

Did you know?

When the Capitol was recently being remodeled, the silver-plated cornerstone laid by George Washington could not be found—even with metal detectors. No one knows where it is.

THE WAR OF 1812 AND BEYOND

It wasn't very long after the Capitol, the White House, and other new buildings were built that the new nation went to war again with Great Britain, and this time the enemy soldiers set them on fire. The buildings probably would have been completely destroyed, but a rainstorm came to their rescue. It was followed by a windstorm so violent that several houses caved in, cannons were blown over, and 30

HISTORY CROSSWORD PUZZLE

1. Colonial men shaved their heads and wore these kinds of wigs.
2. Colonial boys wore these until they were 4 or 5 years old.
3. Students used to write with lumps of this.
4. Indians taught the colonists how to grow and eat this.
5. They taught the first European settlers how to live in the wilderness.
6. The framework of the U.S. government was set down in this document.
7. Colonists used it for money.
8. The North wanted to free them; the South didn't.
9. Pierre L'Enfant chose a hill for its site.

(Answers on page 145)

British soldiers were killed. The British, who were losing the war, fled and the city began rebuilding itself.

The next major crisis of this growing nation was the Civil War, which pitted the North, which wanted to free the slaves, against the South, which needed the slave labor to harvest its crops. The nation's capital became a headquarters for Northern troops. The Capitol Building was turned into a food warehouse, bakery, and sleeping quarters for soldiers. Thousands of slaves fled their plantations and came to this city to be free. To this day, African-Americans make up nearly three-quarters of the population of Washington, D.C.

THE NATION'S CAPITAL TODAY

When the Civil War was over in 1865, the city once again patched up its damage and continued to grow as the country's capital. From 14,000 residents in 1800, the district's population has climbed to about 750,000 today. The larger Washington metropolitan area, which includes parts of Virginia and Maryland, has a population of 4.5 million.

Did you know?

Julia Ward Howe was inspired to write "The Battle Hymn of the Republic" during the Civil War while watching Union soldiers from the Willard Hotel near the White House.

Test yourself

Q: During the Civil War a nurse named Clara Barton tended the wounded in the Capitol. What famous health organization did she later found?

A: The Red Cross.

There aren't only Americans in Washington, D.C. People from all over the world live here, too. Almost every country has a representative in Washington, D.C., and many foreigners come here to study or do business. There are important schools for government and international politics, and a great deal of scientific research is done in this city. As you can probably guess, there are more news reporters here than anywhere else, too. Newspapers, radio, and television stations gather and send news all around the world from our nation's capital.

Washington, D.C., is a huge and important city, but it doesn't look like most big cities in the United States. Why? Look at the buildings. There are no skyscrapers! That's because there is a rule against building most structures taller than 13 stories so that the dome of the Capitol can be seen above everything else.

The Government Today

Did you know?

According to a popular rumor, the White House got its name after British troops burned it in 1814—when the ugly, blackened ruins were painted white. This is not true. The White House was always white.

Today Washington bustles with activity. Each day about 345,000 people go to work here for the federal government. That's more people than live in the entire city of Buffalo, New York.

THE WHITE HOUSE

The most famous government employee is, of course, the president. The president and first lady live at 1600 Pennsylvania Avenue. Their elegant home was not always called the *White House*. It was originally called the *President's House*. A short time later newspapers

29

started calling it the *White House* because of its white walls. But it wasn't until 1903 that President Theodore Roosevelt had all the letterheads changed from *Executive Mansion* to *The White House.*

On a tour of the White House, you will see very few of its 132 rooms. But you *will* see the most historic ones—the Green Room, Blue Room, Red Room, the State Dining Room, and the East Room. The East Room is where the president holds his press conferences. In it hangs a famous portrait of George Washington. First Lady Dolley Madison saved the painting during the War of 1812 when the British burned down the White House. It has been in the White House longer than anything else.

Did you know?

Today, books of matches used in the White House still say *The President's House,* not *The White House.*

■ ■ ■

George Washington is the only president who never lived in the White House. He died the year before it was finished.

The 54 rooms upstairs are off-limits to visitors. They contain lots of storage areas and the living quarters of the president and first lady—about 8 rooms. The Red, Green, and Blue Rooms you see downstairs are used by the president only for entertaining guests.

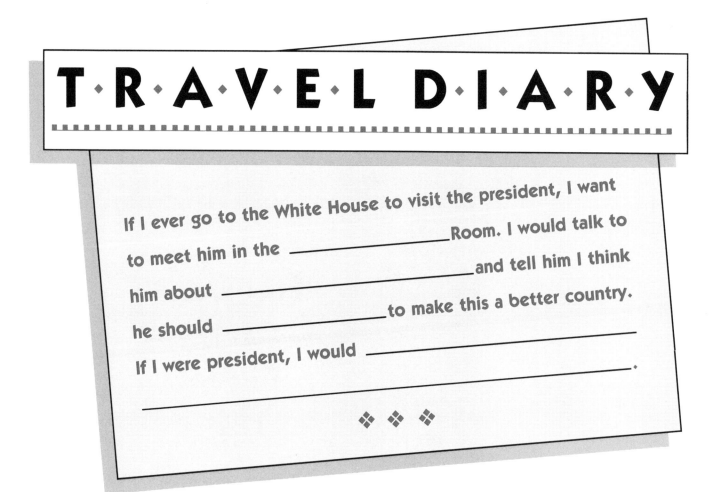

T·R·A·V·E·L D·I·A·R·Y

If I ever go to the White House to visit the president, I want

to meet him in the _____ Room. I would talk to

him about _____ and tell him I think

he should _____ to make this a better country.

If I were president, I would _____

_____.

❖ ❖ ❖

As you tour, you'll pass displays of special china used by different presidents. You'll also see Jacqueline Kennedy's famous rose garden. Notice the seals of the 13 colonies on the walls and ceiling near the entry to the grand staircase on the east side of the White House. Can you find the brass plaque in the Grand Foyer bearing the 4 dates that major White House building took place?

The halls are lined with portraits of former presidents and first ladies. When you reach the painting of John F. Kennedy in the North Foyer, note that his bowed head seems to follow you wherever you go.

31

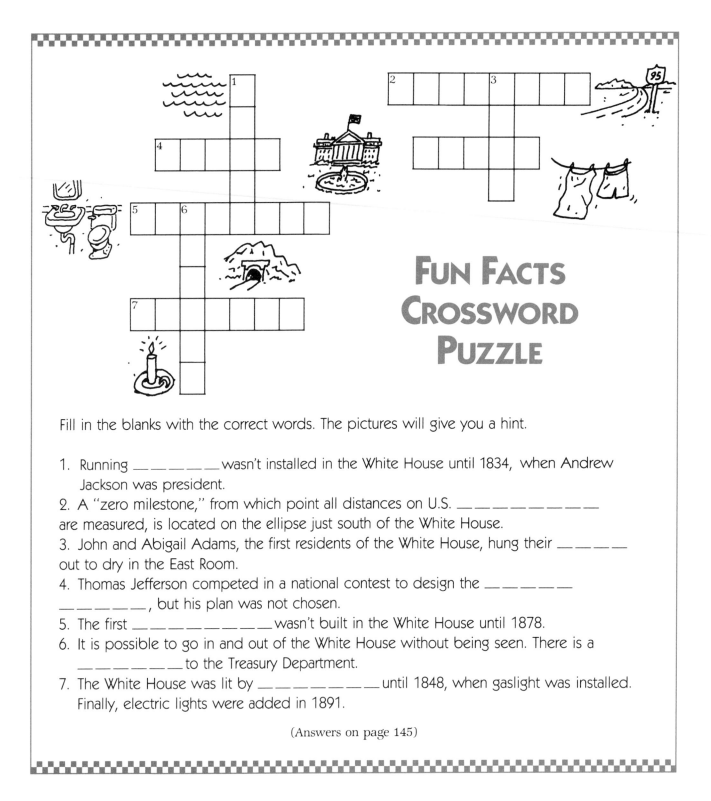

FUN FACTS CROSSWORD PUZZLE

Fill in the blanks with the correct words. The pictures will give you a hint.

1. Running _ _ _ _ _ wasn't installed in the White House until 1834, when Andrew Jackson was president.
2. A "zero milestone," from which point all distances on U.S. _ _ _ _ _ _ _ _ _ are measured, is located on the ellipse just south of the White House.
3. John and Abigail Adams, the first residents of the White House, hung their _ _ _ _ _ _ out to dry in the East Room.
4. Thomas Jefferson competed in a national contest to design the _ _ _ _ _ _ _ _ _ _ _ _ _, but his plan was not chosen.
5. The first _ _ _ _ _ _ _ _ _ _ wasn't built in the White House until 1878.
6. It is possible to go in and out of the White House without being seen. There is a _ _ _ _ _ _ _ _ to the Treasury Department.
7. The White House was lit by _ _ _ _ _ _ _ _ until 1848, when gaslight was installed. Finally, electric lights were added in 1891.

(Answers on page 145)

THE CAPITOL

The White House is the oldest public building in Washington, D.C. The Capitol is the second oldest. It became the seat of the government when lawmakers moved here from Philadelphia in 1800. Now, more than 11,000 new laws are proposed each year by senators and representatives.

Did you know?

The city that is the "seat of government" for a state or nation is called its *capital*. The building in which lawmakers meet is the *capitol*. The building where the lawmakers of the U.S. meet is called the *Capitol*.

There are 2 senators from each state, regardless of its size. The number of representatives each state has depends on the state's population. For instance, tiny Delaware has only 2 representatives, while California has 52. Senators and representatives meet in separate rooms, called *chambers*, in the Capitol. Together they are called *Congress*.

There are good free tours every day, but write your legislator well in advance of your visit for a VIP tour. In fact, you might be able to meet with your senator or representative in person in one of the 6 legislative office buildings next to the Capitol. If you haven't written, drop by his or her office anyway for tickets that will let you observe the Senate or House of Representatives in action, if they are in session. Then head back to the Capitol on the underground train that links the office buildings to the Capitol.

You can find out in advance if Congress is in session by telephoning the Capitol. But why not surprise your

Did you know?

VIP means *Very Important Person.*

T·R·A·V·E·L D·I·A·R·Y

If I ran for office, I would want to be elected to represent _____ in the

the state of _____. I would introduce

_____ so that

a bill to _____. My favorite part of the

_____, because _____

Capitol is the _____.

_____ ❖ ❖ ❖

Did you know?

The cast-iron dome of the Capitol will expand and contract as much as 4 inches on days of temperature extremes.

parents with another method? Whenever the House or Senate is meeting, a flag flies over that chamber. And at night, a 20-foot lantern on the roof is lit when either is in session.

The Capitol has a long history. Its most famous feature is the iron dome on top, which weighs 9 million pounds and is the third largest in the world. The inside of the dome, or *rotunda*, was painted with scenes from American history. The artist painted someone's face (perhaps his own) in a tree trunk on one of the panels. Can you find it?

From the rotunda, head toward the House of Representatives side of the Capitol. You will pass through Statuary Hall. This hall has statues of prominent people donated by various states. See if you can find your state's hero.

Did you know?

The coffins of several American heroes have rested in the Capitol rotunda before burial, including those of 4 murdered presidents: Abraham Lincoln, James Garfield, William McKinley, and John F. Kennedy.

■ ■ ■

The only time the Capitol has been open all night long was when John F. Kennedy's casket lay there—the line of mourners stretched for several blocks.

At one time, representatives met in this room. Ask a guide to demonstrate the mysterious echo. John Quincy Adams's desk sat on a spot where he could hear whispered discussions of the opposing party on the far side of the room. The story goes that he kept this secret and surprised everyone when he seemed to guess what the other side was going to do before they did it. Find the plaque on the floor marking where Adams suffered a fatal stroke. Other plaques mark the seats of legislators—including Abraham Lincoln, who went on to become president.

Did you know?

The acoustics were so bad in Statuary Hall, the original chamber of the House of Representatives, that massive red curtains were hung to help muffle the echoes.

Near the House chambers, climb the same stone spiral staircase British troops climbed when they set fire to the Capitol during the War of 1812.

Can you find the bloodstains on the marble stairs leading to the White House Press Gallery? This was where, in 1890, a congressman was shot to death by a newspaper reporter during an argument about some articles the reporter had written.

Today the U.S. House of Representatives is the largest legislative chamber in the world. The leader, called the *Speaker of the House*, faces a semicircle of seats. There are no assigned seats, but Democrats always sit to his right and Republicans to his left.

Likewise, in the Senate, Democrats sit to the right and Republicans to the left of the vice president. But Senate seats are assigned.

Notice the saltshaker-like bottles on the desks of the hundred senators. They once contained sand, which was used to blot ink. Many of the Senate desks date back to the early 1800s when the Capitol was rebuilt after being burned in the war. Many bear the initials of the legislators who sat in them. Jefferson Davis's desk has a patch on the side where a Union soldier struck it with a bayonet. Daniel Webster's desk has a detachable writing box on top.

Did you know?

When the House is in session, a silver inkstand is placed on the Speaker's table. This same stand has been put out since 1818.

████████████████████████████████████

HELPFUL HINT

Bells ring out codes that let legislators throughout the Capitol and legislative office buildings know what's going on in chambers. Lights under clocks also flash the same message. This will help you to decode them:

Senate

1 ring or light	yeas and nays vote
2 rings or lights	quorum call
3 rings or lights	call of absentees
4 rings or lights	adjournment
5 rings or lights	halfway through a vote
6 rings or lights	recess

House

1 ring or light	teller vote
2 rings or lights	recorded vote
3 rings or lights	quorum call
4 rings or lights	adjournment
5 rings or lights	quick 5-minute vote (normal votes are 15 minutes)
6 rings or lights	recess

Boxes filled with snuff, a form of tobacco popular years ago, still sit on ledges near the Senate speakers' platform. No one admits to using the snuff today, yet workers are always having to refill the boxes.

Do you see the people, ages 14 to 16, delivering messages in the 2 chambers? They are called *pages*, and you could become one. They attend a special school in the Library of Congress from 6:30 A.M. until about 10:00 A.M., then run to the Capitol to work while Congress is in session. To become a page, you need to apply with your senator or representative. The competition is tough—fewer than a hundred pages are chosen each year.

THE SUPREME COURT

Until 1935 the Supreme Court, the highest court in the nation, met in the Capitol. It now has its own building across the street. You can't miss it. The building has 16 columns of white Vermont marble 3 stories high and 4 bronze doors that together weigh 26 tons.

In most courts there is only 1 judge. But the Supreme Court has 9 judges, called *justices*, who together decide cases. From October through April, the court is in session Mondays through Wednesdays for 2 weeks, then switches to private meetings for the next 2 weeks (except for winter vacations). In May and June the justices hear no new cases, but meet to announce decisions.

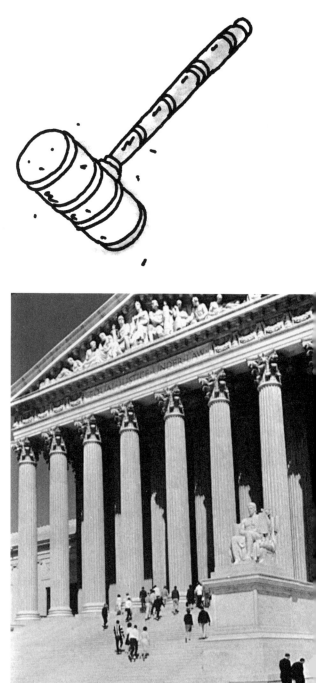

Test yourself

Q: Who was the first woman to sit on the Supreme Court?

A: Sandra Day O'Connor, who was appointed by President Reagan in 1981.

The job of the Supreme Court justices is to apply the Constitution to new situations and decide if decisions made by lower courts, by Congress, and by the president are in keeping with the principles of the Constitution.

If you want to see the court in action, it's a good idea to arrive well before 10:00 A.M. since the chamber holds less than 200 observers.

Did you know?

Several thousand cases are brought to the Supreme Court each year. But the justices select only about 150 for consideration.

First the marshal opens the session, then the justices, dressed in black robes, file in. The chief justice sits in the center. Note the different styles of chairs—justices design their own chairs, and when a justice retires, the others buy the chair for him or her as a parting gift.

Tradition is very important in this court. White feather pens are still placed on the lawyers' tables every day, even though no one uses them anymore.

On days when the court is not in session, a guide gives a lecture every hour on the half hour explaining how the court operates. A movie on the ground floor runs whether court is in session or not.

THE LIBRARY OF CONGRESS

The Library of Congress is next door to the Supreme Court. This is the official library for U.S. legislators. Each year the library workers handle more than 300,000 inquiries from members of Congress and their staffs as well as from other branches of government. But that isn't their only task.

T·R·A·V·E·L D·I·A·R·Y

I read _____ books a month. My favorite book is _____

_____. It's about _____

_____.

Some of the neat things I saw at the Library of Congress

were _____.

❖ ❖ ❖

Did you know?

The Library of Congress collection grows by 10 items a minute.

■ ■ ■

If you spent 1 minute looking at each item in the Library of Congress for 8 hours a day, 5 days a week, it would take you 648 years to see everything.

Another job is to assign library card catalog numbers to books. The library is also where all books, sheet music, film scripts, and other documents in America are copyrighted to protect them from being copied.

The Library of Congress is the largest library in the world. It has more than 83 million items, including books, magazines, manuscripts, photos, music, recordings, films, and maps. If the shelves were laid end to end, they would stretch from Washington, D.C., to Detroit, Michigan.

The Great Hall through which you enter is breathtaking with its fancy dome, statues, murals, inlaid floor, carvings, and columns. When the

building was completed in the early 1900s, it was described as the "most beautiful building in the world."

Many historic documents are preserved here, including Thomas Jefferson's rough draft of the Declaration of Independence, letters written by George Washington, and Lincoln's Gettysburg Address, as well as the contents of his pockets the night he died. There are diaries and notebooks kept by Alexander Graham Bell, who invented the telephone; magic scrapbooks of Houdini; the walking stick of writer Charles Dickens; and personal papers of comedian Groucho Marx and other famous people.

The library has the smallest book ever printed. It's called *Ant* and is about the size of—you guessed it— an ant. You've probably heard of Stradivarius violins—the finest in the world. Well, the Library of Congress has one of those, too.

Did you know?

Four hundred seventy languages appear in the library's collection.

■ ■ ■

The Library of Congress produces more than 2 million books a year in special print for the blind and physically handicapped.

These valuable items are not on display, but people doing research can study them. One priceless item that *is* on exhibit is the original copy of the Gutenberg Bible, the first book ever printed in movable type.

Famous Documents

Do you know what the missing words are to the famous lines
of these historical documents?

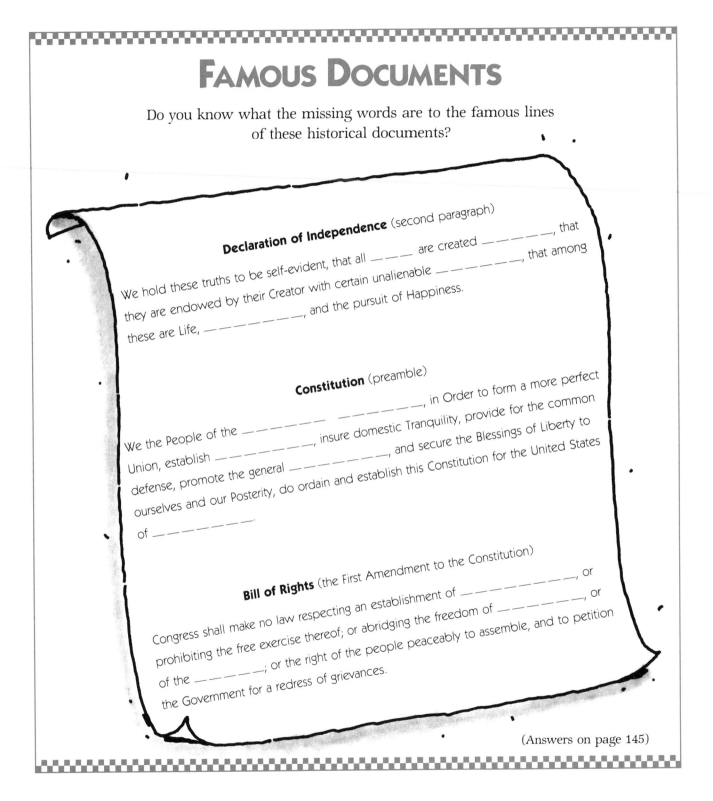

Declaration of Independence (second paragraph)

We hold these truths to be self-evident, that all _____ are created _____, that they are endowed by their Creator with certain unalienable _____, that among these are Life, _____, and the pursuit of Happiness.

Constitution (preamble)

We the People of the _____ _____, in Order to form a more perfect Union, establish _____, insure domestic Tranquility, provide for the common defense, promote the general _____, and secure the Blessings of Liberty to ourselves and our Posterity, do ordain and establish this Constitution for the United States of _____.

Bill of Rights (the First Amendment to the Constitution)

Congress shall make no law respecting an establishment of _____, or prohibiting the free exercise thereof; or abridging the freedom of _____, or of the _____; or the right of the people peaceably to assemble, and to petition the Government for a redress of grievances.

(Answers on page 145)

THE NATIONAL ARCHIVES

You can see the original Declaration of Independence, as well as the U.S. Bill of Rights and the Constitution. They're in the National Archives. These documents are so old that the ink is faded. To preserve them, they are kept in helium-filled glass cases and lowered 22 feet into underground chambers at night.

The National Archives is sometimes called the *national memory* because it houses all of the nation's official paperwork. Here papers are sorted out and decisions are made to store or destroy them. Patents, census and immigration records, pension files, photographs, treaties, motion pictures, and other documents dating as far back as 1775 can be found here. You must be over 16 years old to get permission to do research, though.

The National Archives is also famous for genealogical research. (Geneaology is the study of family trees.) Here you can trace your family back to discover where your ancestors were from and who you are related to. You may be surprised to find some important historical figures in your family!

Did you know?

The National Archives and its branches store some 1.3 million cubic feet of historical records, including former president Nixon's Watergate tapes.

■ ■ ■

Author Alex Haley began his work on *Roots* here.

Can you fill in your family tree? How far can you go back in your family? Do you know all the names of your grandparents? How about those of your great-grandparents?

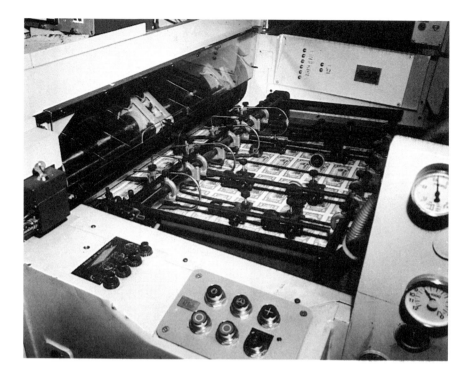

THE BUREAU OF ENGRAVING AND PRINTING

This is where the money is—oodles and oodles of it. Every day about $22.5 million is manufactured here by 2,300 people working around the clock in shifts, 6 days a week. Notice the security guards and cameras watching you.

Most of the money made is used to replace worn-out bills. The $1, $5, and $10 bills are printed every day. The $20 bills are printed less often, and $50 and $100 bills are made only once a year during a 3-month period. Bills of larger sizes—$500, $1,000, $5,000, and $10,000—have not been printed since 1969 because there are already enough.

Did you know?

The Bureau of Engraving prints $71 billion a year.

Through a series of windows you can watch the bills being made. Large sheets of special "paper" are pressed under engraved steel plates coated with secret-formula ink. On one day the green ink side of bills is printed and on the next, the black ink side. Each large sheet contains 32 bills. Watch as the printed sheets roll off the press in stacks of 10,000. Each stack of $1 bills is worth $320,000. The sheets are then cut apart and each bill is studied for defects. Making a $1 bill takes 3 to 5 days from start to finish.

Test yourself

Q: What is the life expectancy of a $1 bill?

A: With normal usage, 18 months. A $5 bill lasts 2 years, a $10 bill lasts 5 years, and a $100 bill will be around for 23 years.

∎ ∎ ∎

Q: Why is there no demand for $500 or $1000 bills nowadays?

A: With credit cards and checks available, people have no need to carry such large sums of money.

∎ ∎ ∎

Q: Each bill contains fibers of 2 colors. Take a close look. What are they?

A: Red and blue.

Did you know?

No trees have been cut down to make dollar bills. They are not made of paper. They are made of cloth—75 percent cotton and 25 percent linen.

See the Bureau of Engraving's display of counterfeit money, a $100,000 bill (the largest bill ever printed), and money no longer in use. Don't be disappointed that coins are not made here. That's the job of the Bureaus of the Mint in Philadelphia and Denver. If you want coins that haven't ever been used, go to the Treasury Department's Cash Room next to the White House.

The Bureau of Engraving and Printing doesn't only print money. Thirty-six billion postage stamps a year are printed here, as well as identification badges, treasury bonds, and even White House invitations.

Pretend that you're the president and design the invitation below for a special party. And since you're the president, you can also design your very own postage stamp.

Did you know?

Every year the Bureau of Engraving uses 4.8 million pounds of "paper" and $14 million worth of ink.

▪ ▪ ▪

If the U.S. treasurer stays in office for 5 years, his or her signature will be on 5.8 billion dollar bills.

Think about this: if you had all the money the Bureau of Engraving printed in 1 year and spent $1 every second, it would take you 225 years to go broke. Wow!

THE FEDERAL BUREAU OF INVESTIGATION

They say the FBI tour is at the top of every kid's "10 Most Wanted" list of things to do in Washington, D.C. And with good reason. Solving mysterious deaths, tracking down murderers from a few threads of cloth or the dirt on a suspect's shoe, and catching spies are all in a day's work at the FBI.

Some of the scenes you've seen on TV will come to life in FBI labs. There is a document room, where handwriting is analyzed to detect forgery, ransom notes are studied, shredded or burned documents are pieced together, and shoe prints and tire tracks are identified. There is even a file of notes once used by thieves to demand cash during bank robberies.

In another lab, hairs and fibers are studied. The FBI can tell if a hair is that of a human or an animal, if it was a woman or man, if the hair was pulled out or fell out, what part of the body it was from, the race of the person, and sometimes even the person's blood type. Another lab is used to check out bloodstains.

If there has been a hit-and-run car accident, the FBI is able to study auto paint samples as small as a pinhead to identify the make and model of the car.

Fingerprints of 60 million people are on file here. Some are used by the FBI to identify criminals, but many are for people working in government or high-security jobs. Perhaps the fingerprints of someone in your family are here—1 out of every 4 Americans' fingerprints are.

See pictures of the "10 Most Wanted" criminals in America. And hear stories about the most infamous gangsters in U.S. history—Pretty Boy Floyd, Baby Face Nelson, Al Capone, and John Dillinger.

Fill in the "Wanted" poster any way you like. The "criminal" could be your sister, brother, friend, or enemy. It could even be you!

WANTED

Name: _____

Description: _____

_____

Crime: _____

7008721 39661

DRAW YOUR THUMBPRINT

Look closely at the lines in your thumb—they're different from the lines in everyone else's. Draw a picture of what they look like.

Did you know?

Only 7 women have ever appeared on the FBI's "Most Wanted" list—all since 1950.

Learn how the FBI deals with white-collar crime, terrorism, kidnapping, organized crime, and spying. Listen to how it solved famous cases such as the "lemonade" case, in which 2 Soviet spies trying to get top-secret data from a navy man used a lemonade package as a signal.

You'll also see clever devices to hide microfilm that have been taken away from spies: a hollow nail, a fake pencil, a dummy nickel, a doll, even a hollowed-out tree branch. Don't miss the weapons room, where you'll see the guns used to commit many crimes, including a rifle like the one Lee Harvey Oswald used to kill John F. Kennedy.

But what most kids like best comes at the end of the tour. A life-size paper target is "killed" by an FBI agent in a burst of submachine gun fire. If you write to the FBI and ask for one of these paper targets, you will receive one free.

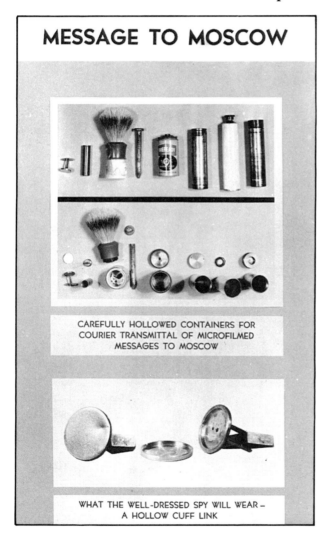

MESSAGE TO MOSCOW

CAREFULLY HOLLOWED CONTAINERS FOR COURIER TRANSMITTAL OF MICROFILMED MESSAGES TO MOSCOW

WHAT THE WELL-DRESSED SPY WILL WEAR — A HOLLOW CUFF LINK

Did you know?

By the end of your tour, 2 people will have been murdered and more than 60 robberies committed in the U.S. Look for more bad news on the FBI's crime clock.

Glimpses of the Famous

When you think of Washington, D.C., you can't help but think of George Washington, Thomas Jefferson, Abraham Lincoln, John F. Kennedy, and all the other famous presidents who have led this country. Your visit will give you a chance to learn more about the lives of these great men.

GEORGE WASHINGTON

How about a firsthand look at the teeth of George Washington? They're not made out of wood as commonly believed, but out of an ivory tusk. A replica is on display at the **Museum of American History**—one of the many museums along the Mall, which stretches from the Capitol to the Washington Monument. George Washington's revolutionary war uniform and field headquarters tent are also in the museum.

Other than the name of the capital itself, the most famous memorial to Washington is the **Washington Monument.** It towers 555 feet over the Mall and is the world's tallest masonry structure. At its base, the marble walls are 15 feet thick. The monument was planned in 1783, but Washington never got to see this majestic tower. Building didn't start until 1848, nearly 50 years after our first president's death, and it wasn't completed until 1884. If you look closely, you'll notice the color of the marble changes about 150 feet from the base of the monument. This was the height of the tower when work stopped for 22 years before and during the Civil War. When building resumed, the marble came from another level of the quarry.

Did you know?

The Washington Monument sways one-eighth of an inch in a 35 mph wind.

There are a whopping 897 steps to the top of the Washington Monument, but visitors aren't allowed to walk up them. They have to take the elevator instead. That takes 70 seconds—a far shorter time than the original steam elevator ride that lasted 20 minutes. The view from the top is perhaps the best of all Washington, D.C. The Capitol is to the east, the White House to the north, the Jefferson Memorial to the south, and the Lincoln Memorial to the west.

Test yourself

Q: The Washington Monument used to have 898 steps to climb. Today it has only 897. How come?

A: The bottom one was made into a wheelchair ramp.

For fear of vandalism, park officials only allow visitors to walk down the stairs at 10:00 A.M. and 2:00 P.M. Saturdays and Sundays, when special "Down the Steps" tours are given if staff is available. You'll see various carvings on the inside walls, a piece of stone from the famous Parthenon temple in Greece, and writings honoring private citizens, states, nations, and clubs that donated marble blocks.

THOMAS JEFFERSON

Another monument to another great president is a must to visit. That is the **Jefferson Memorial**. Its columns and dome echo the style Thomas Jefferson used to design his own home, Monticello, and the rotunda at the University of Virginia. The interior of the dome bears famous writings of Jefferson, our third president and an author of the Declaration of Independence. A 19-foot, 5-ton bronze statue of this great champion of religious and racial freedom stands in the center. National Park guards are there to answer questions and give tours on request. The most thrilling time to visit is in the evening, when this pillared monument overlooking the tidal basin is brightly lit.

Did you know?

Women and children weren't allowed to ride in the first steam elevator to the top of the Washington Monument because it was thought to be unsafe.

T·R·A·V·E·L D·I·A·R·Y

The monuments in Washington, D.C., are _____.

The prettiest monument I've seen is the _____. The biggest I've

seen is the _____. My favorite

of all the monuments I've seen in Washington is the _____

_____, because _____

_____.

❖ ❖ ❖

ABRAHAM LINCOLN

You can see the gun that killed President Lincoln, bone fragments from his skull, and the room in which he died on April 15, 1865. Start near the Capitol at **Ford's Theatre,** where actor John Wilkes Booth shot President Lincoln. See the box seat where Lincoln sat that fateful night, then go downstairs to where the **Lincoln Museum** has the clothing he wore when he was shot, the flag that draped his coffin, and Booth's gun and riding boot (slit down the side because he broke his leg during his escape). Read Booth's own diary explaining why he killed Lincoln, whom he blamed for the Civil War: "I can never repent it, although we hated to kill. Our country owed all her trouble to him [Lincoln], and God simply made me the instrument of his punishment."

Across the street in the **Petersen House,** often called the *House Where Lincoln Died*, is the actual bloodstained pillow that lay under Lincoln's head. To see the skull fragments and the bullet that killed Lincoln, you need to go to the **Armed Forces Medical Museum** in the Walter Reed Army Medical Center. This unusual museum also has a collection of microscopes, early X-ray equipment, and pickled body parts, including the amputated leg of Civil War general Daniel Sickles.

Test yourself

Q: A plaster cast of Lincoln's right hand at the Armed Forces Medical Museum shows that it was bigger than his left. Can you guess why?

A: His hand was swollen from frequent handshaking during the election campaign.

Did you know?

Strangely, a few weeks before he shot President Lincoln, John Wilkes Booth rented the same room in the Petersen House and slept in the same bed where Lincoln later died.

There is another place honoring Lincoln that you can't miss—the **Lincoln Memorial.** It's at the west end of the long, narrow reflecting pool that runs to the Washington Monument. It has 36 marble columns, one for each state in the Union at the time Lincoln died, and 56 steps, one for each year Lincoln was alive. Inside, Lincoln sits larger than life. Lincoln was 6 feet 4 inches tall, but this statue is 19 feet high and weighs 150 tons. Engraved in the walls are Lincoln's famous Gettysburg Address and his second inaugural address. What few people know is that there is a cave under the Lincoln Memorial. Special "Under the Lincoln" tours are given in spring and fall. But they're very popular, and you need to contact the National Parks Service weeks in advance to sign up.

Did you know?

The reflecting pool is nearly 2,000 feet long.

JOHN F. KENNEDY
■ ■ ■ ■ ■ ■ ■ ■ ■ ■ ■ ■ ■ ■ ■ ■

There is a living memorial to one of our more recent former presidents. The **John F. Kennedy Center for the Performing Arts,** opened in 1971, is our national cultural center. There are 5 different theaters in this gigantic center—the Concert Hall, Opera House, Eisenhower Theater, American Film Institute, and the Terrace Theater—where you can see performances by the best musical, theater, and dance groups from around the world.

Did you know?

There are 3 restaurants in the Kennedy Center, ranging from a cafeteria to a deluxe restaurant.

■ ■ ■

The Washington Monument could be placed on its side in the Grand Foyer and still have 75 feet to spare!

■ ■ ■

Italy donated the 3,700 tons of marble used in the building.

There's a lot to see here even if you don't go to a performance. Take a free 50-minute tour, or explore it on your own. Make sure you visit the Hall of Nations, where all the flags of countries recognized by the U.S. are displayed in alphabetical order, and the Hall of States, which is lined with the flags of the 50 states and 4 territories, hung in the same order in which they joined the Union. In the red-carpeted Grand Foyer you can see a 7-foot bronze bust of John F. Kennedy. Many countries gave incredible gifts to the center in memory of Kennedy, such as the crystal chandeliers from Sweden and Austria, the gold silk stage curtains from Japan, the beautiful tapestries from different African countries, and an alabaster vase about 4,500 years old from Egypt.

If you want to go to a show, you have many choices. There are special performances of music, dance, plays, mimes, and puppets on some Saturdays just for kids, and they're usually free. The regular programs include symphonies, operas, plays, movies, music concerts (from jazz to pop), and special tribute ceremonies.

T·R·A·V·E·L D·I·A·R·Y

If I played a musical instrument, I would play the _____

_____, because _____.

_____ music.

I would play _____

If I could see anyone perform at the Kennedy Center, I'd like

_____, because

to see _____.

_____

❖ ❖ ❖

MANY GREAT AMERICANS— KNOWN AND UNKNOWN

Did you know?

Three of the first 5 presidents died on July 4—Thomas Jefferson, John Adams, and James Monroe.

John F. Kennedy and many other U.S. heroes are honored nearby in the most famous cemetery in the country—**Arlington National Cemetery.** It is in Virginia, just across the Potomac River from the Lincoln Memorial.

A flame burns constantly at Kennedy's grave. In a visit to the former mansion of Civil War general Robert E. Lee, which overlooks the cemetery, President Kennedy was once overheard remarking about the peaceful feeling he had there. "I could stay here forever," he said. Near Kennedy's grave is the grave of his brother, Senator Robert Kennedy, who was also killed by an assassin.

You'll find the graves of other famous people here as well—President William Howard Taft; Pierre L'Enfant, the first city planner; Abner Doubleday, the founder of baseball; boxer Joe Louis; Virgil Grissom, Edward White, and Roger Chaffee, the three astronauts killed in a 1967 test spacecraft explosion; Supreme Court justices Oliver Wendell Holmes, William O. Douglas, and Earl Warren; Audie Murphy, the most decorated hero of World War II; and astronauts Mike Smith and Dick Scobee, who died in the 1986 explosion of the *Challenger*.

Perhaps the most moving monuments of all are those for the less famous who have given their lives for this country. While in Arlington National Cemetery, stop by the **Tomb of the Unknown Soldier**, dedicated to those killed in World Wars I and II and the Korean War, but whose bodies could not be identified.

Just north of the cemetery is another famous war memorial—a statue showing marines raising the U.S. flag at Iwo Jima during World War II.

Back in the Washington, D.C. side of the Potomac, near the Lincoln Memorial, is the **Vietnam Veterans Memorial**. This V-shaped black marble wall simply bearing the 58,022 names of those who were killed in the war or are still missing in action, is a very personal and moving memorial.

Also near the Lincoln Memorial is the equally moving **Korean War Memorial**, dedicated on July 27, 1995. Here you will find 19 larger-than-life sculptures representing brave infantrymen dressed in battle gear. This memorial's inscription reads: "Our nation honors her sons and daughters who answered the call to defend a country they never knew and a people they never met."

The Mall and Mr. Smithson

Washington has some of the greatest museums in the world. And it's all thanks to a man who never even visited America.

James Smithson was an Englishman dedicated to learning. In 1829 he willed the U.S. government $500,000 to be used to expand knowledge. As a result, the Smithsonian Institution was founded. Several of the Smithsonian's museums line the Mall near the Capitol and can be visited on the same day.

MUSEUM OF NATURAL HISTORY

Climb aboard the giant dinosaur named Uncle Beazley on the Mall outside the Museum of Natural History. This creature is just a hint of what's to come. As you enter the museum you'll meet a gigantic, 12-ton African bush elephant (stuffed, of course). It is the largest elephant ever taken from Africa.

Did you know?

The earliest evidence of life is 3,500 million years old. To see it, look in the Earliest Evidence of Life Hall.

PLACES TO VISIT

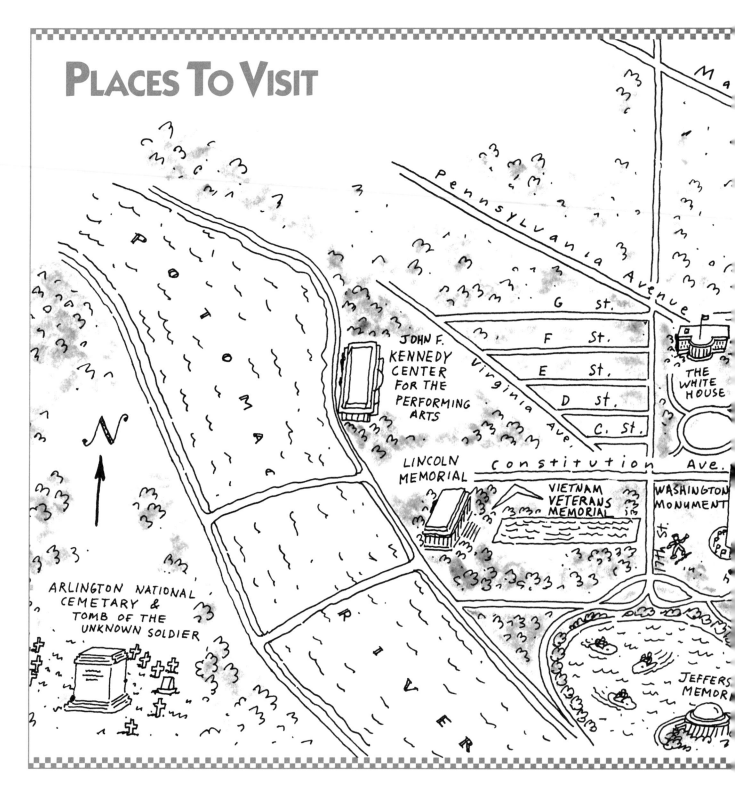

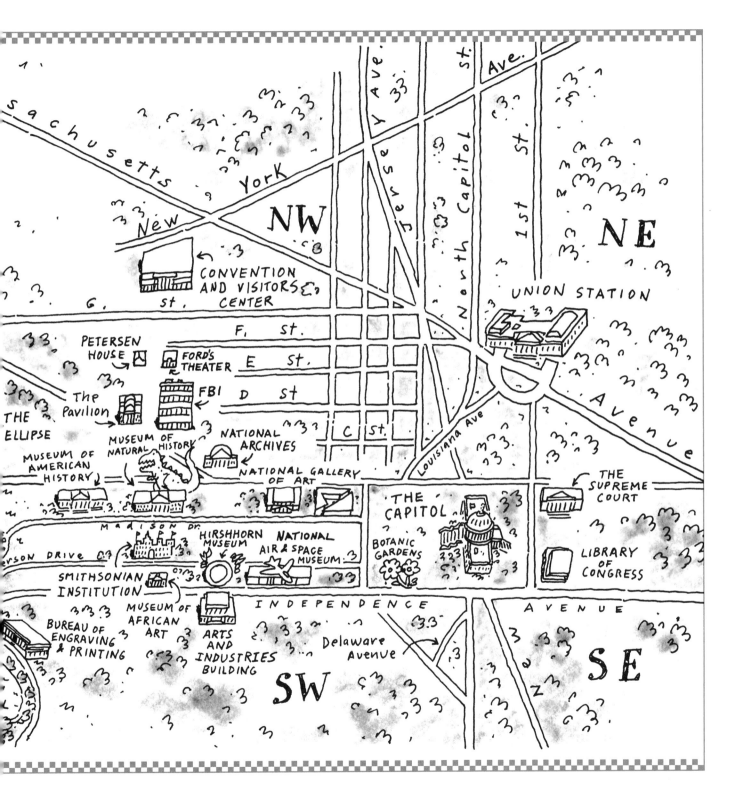

Test yourself

In the dinosaur room, see if you can find a prehistoric fish that has swallowed another fish.

- - -

Q: What is the biggest animal that ever lived?

A: The blue whale, which grew to 98 feet in length and 150 tons. See a model at the Museum of Natural History.

- - -

Q: Where does a whale have hair?

A: On its chin. Look at the chin whiskers on the blue whale.

The Dinosaur Gallery to the elephant's right is a treasure house of fossils and prehistoric bones. If you're interested in a huge dinosaur footprint, a dinosaur egg that's 70 million years old, or a plant-eating dinosaur called a *diplodoccus* that was 80 feet long and weighed 25 tons, this is the place for you.

Not far away, take a look at the open jaws wide enough for a Volkswagen to drive through. This is the rebuilt jaw of a great white shark that lived 5 million years ago. Some of the teeth, 5 to 6 inches long, are real. Next, see if you can find the fossil of a 2½-foot camel that used to live, believe it or not, in Nebraska.

If these aren't impressive enough for you, try the "Bone Room," where skeletons of everything from mouse to man are assembled for your viewing pleasure.

Test yourself

Q: How did the gauchos of South America catch a big ostrichlike bird called a *rhea* without guns, nets, or traps?

A: With bolas, long cords with heavy balls at the end.

■ ■ ■

Q: What survives in total darkness 1.5 miles down on the seafloor?

A: Tube worms, which don't need oxygen. They live on sulfides.

If you're squeamish, you may not want to go into the Insect Zoo. There you'll see enough living, creepy-crawly creatures to last a lifetime—gigantic cockroaches, centipedes, tarantulas, beetles, leaf-cutting ants, huge grasshoppers, and hermit crabs, to mention just a few. There are working anthills and beehives, too. Don't miss the prehistoric dragonfly—it has a 5-foot wingspan!

In other parts of the museum you'll see displays of stuffed animals in their natural surroundings. The 11-foot-long Bengal tiger is believed to be the largest ever killed in India.

Other exhibits explain the origin of the earth and its changes through the ages. View the 2-million-year-old skull of a manlike creature from Africa. See various human cultures through the years come alive in scenes showing everyday life. There is even a display of real mummies. One is an eighteenth-century Philadelphia man whose body, strangely, turned into soap.

A highlight of this museum is the Gem and Mineral Room. Any fortune-teller would be jealous that the world's largest crystal ball, more than 12 inches in diameter and 106 pounds, is here. How about wearing a ring the size of the Hope Diamond? It's 45.5 carats and the largest blue diamond in the world. Not big enough? How about a 168-carat emerald? Still bigger? Well, there's a 423-carat blue sapphire. And if that's not enough, you'll be bowled over with a topaz that's nearly the size of a baseball—12,555 carats!

Did you know?

The size of gemstones is always measured in carats. One carat weighs 200 milligrams.

Test yourself

Q: What is the most common color of a topaz?

A: Yellow. (But they can also be white, blue, or green.)

■ ■ ■

Can you find your birthstone in the Gem and Mineral Room?

Here you'll also find the diamond necklace the French emperor Napoleon gave to his wife, Marie Louise; Marie Louise's crown with 950 diamonds; and earrings worn by French queen Marie Antoinette before she was beheaded during the French Revolution.

Nearby are rocks of a far different sort—moon rocks, meteorites from outer space, and pieces of the world's oldest-known rocks, formed nearly 3.8 billion years before man.

Try timing your visit between 10:30 A.M. and 3:30 P.M. Friday through Sunday, or between noon and 2:30 P.M. Tuesday through Thursday. That's when the first-floor Discovery Room is open. This room features hands-on exhibits and games. Handle mastodon teeth, a crocodile head, fossils, a stuffed porcupine, a snakeskin, coral, and bones. Examine minerals under microscopes. Play drums from Kenya or dress in foreign costumes. When you've had your fill, go next door to the Museum of American History.

MUSEUM OF AMERICAN HISTORY

There are two amazing sights as you enter the Museum of American History from the Mall. One is the continually moving Foucault Pendulum. This brass ball suspended from the ceiling swings forever across the same spot, yet one by one it knocks down red blocks arranged like dominoes in a circle. Can you guess why? The floor under the pendulum is actually moving because the earth is rotating.

Did you know?

The Foucault Pendulum was named after Jean Foucault, a French physicist. This is a copy of one he designed.

Betsy Ross has always been credited with sewing the first American flag. Actually, there is no evidence to back this up, although we do know that she made flags for the Pennsylvania navy in 1777.

You may have to wait a bit for the next item. It can only be seen every hour on the hour. It's the original star-spangled banner—the flag that flew over Fort McHenry in Baltimore during the British attack in the War of 1812. It inspired Francis Scott Key to write our national anthem. Because the tattered flag is so old and delicate, it is hidden behind a curtain except for viewing times.

This museum has some very special exhibits, but you have to hunt for them. See if you can find the ruby slippers Judy Garland wore in *The Wizard of Oz*, the leather jacket worn by Fonzie on TV's "Happy Days," jazz king Dizzy Gillespie's trumpet, J.R.'s hat from TV's "Dallas," the boxing gloves of Muhammad Ali and Joe Louis, and the eyeglasses Christopher Reeve wore as Clark Kent in the movie *Superman*.

Boxing gloves   Muhammad Ali

Someone got into the Museum of American History and moved all of the exhibits around. Help the curator (that's the person in charge of the museum) find the exhibits.

```
A  T  S  G  F  I  R  E  W  A  G  O  N  E  R
T  R  U  M  P  E  T  F  C  J  R  T  W  Y  O
S  E  Q  P  S  U  Y  O  X  U  N  R  V  E  M
W  N  R  H  M  I  P  U  Q  M  U  U  D  G  E
A  N  E  O  L  O  G  C  A  B  I  N  M  L  P
L  A  C  T  L  N  W  A  Z  U  C  K  I  A  E
K  B  O  B  O  T  K  U  F  R  Q  K  C  S  Z
I  D  R  U  B  Y  S  L  I  P  P  E  R  S  E
N  E  D  V  D  X  P  T  C  L  D  Y  O  E  N
G  L  P  S  E  C  V  P  O  U  I  R  P  S  I
S  G  L  Y  M  H  C  E  V  Q  L  E  H  O  G
T  N  A  L  N  A  K  N  E  C  I  W  O  D  N
I  A  Y  F  X  I  G  D  R  O  G  F  N  A  E
C  P  E  P  E  R  J  U  E  T  H  G  E  C  M
K  S  R  T  S  I  L  L  D  T  T  B  U  N  A
Z  R  X  Y  N  O  B  U  W  O  B  H  K  H  E
H  A  T  A  W  Z  K  M  A  N  U  N  B  V  T
D  T  F  B  O  X  I  N  G  G  L  O  V  E  S
H  S  J  I  G  A  C  H  O  I  B  G  A  J  I
M  O  D  E  L  T  J  B  N  N  W  G  M  F  L
```

FOUCAULT PENDULUM   BOXING GLOVES   WALKING STICK   MODEL T
STAR-SPANGLED BANNER   EYEGLASSES   MICROPHONE   STEAM ENGINE
RUBY SLIPPERS   COVERED WAGON   LIGHT BULB   GOWNS
TRUMPET   LOG CABIN   RECORD PLAYER   TRUNK
HAT   FIRE WAGON   COTTON GIN   CHAIR

(Answers on page 146)

The museum is filled with Americana—a genuine covered wagon, a log cabin, a hand-pumped fire wagon, Ben Franklin's walking stick, the microphone Franklin D. Roosevelt used for radio broadcasts, and the passenger section of the jet John F. Kennedy used for campaigning.

Imagine what it must have felt like to be a slave as you look at the iron slave collars and heavy chains they once wore.

Did you know?

A Chippendale chair, which has graceful lines, was named after Thomas Chippendale, an English cabinetmaker.

You'll also see inventions that changed the way Americans live: Thomas Edison's electric light bulb and first record player, Eli Whitney's cotton gin, Henry Ford's Model T car, a real 280-ton steam engine, and an atom smasher.

You're sure to get a kick out of the display of gowns worn by first ladies through the years. Notice how small some of the women were 150 years ago.

Don't miss the Hands-On History Room, where you can explore life in colonial America. Girls can try on corsets and get a lesson in how colonial women were taught to stand. You can build a Chippendale chair, see how cotton cloth was made, make a wooden bucket, walk through a house that hasn't been changed since 1684, and see if you can guess the uses for items in a colonial trunk.

T·R·A·V·E·L D·I·A·R·Y

My favorite part of the Museum of American History is the

_____ , because _____ .

I saw the _____ that belonged to

_____ . The most amazing

_____ .

invention I saw was the _____

The prettiest dress a first lady wore was the _____

that belonged to _____ .

The ugliest dress was _____

❖ ❖ ❖

There are other hands-on areas. In one, you can learn how to make shoes as they did in the early twentieth century after assembly-line production replaced the cobbler. In another, you can trace the development of electricity and learn how a light bulb works. The Spirit of 1776 area re-creates the lifestyle of a soldier in the American Revolution. You can touch his uniform, guns, and equipment.

Did you know?

If you mail your postcards from the old post office in the Museum of American History, they will get a unique *Smithsonian Station* postmark.

Test yourself

Before visiting the National Air and Space Museum, guess the color of the piece of moon rock at the entrance.

NATIONAL AIR AND SPACE MUSEUM

▪▪▪▪▪▪▪▪▪▪▪▪▪▪▪▪▪▪

The story of aviation is best told at the National Air and Space Museum. In one spot you can see everything from the Wright brothers' *Kitty Hawk*, which made man's first sustained flight, to the command module of the *Apollo 11*, which landed on the moon.

You can walk under airplanes, satellites, rockets, and spacecraft that hang from the ceiling. You can walk in and around others.

Of special interest are the *Skylab* Orbital Workshop, which shows how people live in space; a replica of the space shuttle *Columbia*; John Glenn's *Friendship 7*, which made America's first manned flight around the earth; and a golf cart-like vehicle that was driven on the moon.

You can also see a pedal-powered airplane; the plane in which Amelia Earhart flew solo across the Atlantic in 1932; a U-2 spy plane; and a replica of the Soviet's *Sputnik I*, the first satellite in orbit.

See Able, the stuffed monkey, in her space couch, just as the real Able was in test rocket flights in 1959.

A special treat is the SS *Pussiewillow*, a whimsical sculpture of a space vehicle that flaps, gyrates, whirs, and glows.

Don't miss touching the 4-billion-year-old moon rock as you enter the building from the Mall. Yes, it's real.

Did you know?

When Charles Lindbergh flew across the Atlantic solo in 1927, he had to stay awake for more than 33 hours.

T·R·A·V·E·L D·I·A·R·Y

I think NASA should send ——————————— into outer space in a ———————————, because ———————————. The planet I would most like to visit would be ———————————, because ———————————. I think it would look like ———————————.

❖ ❖ ❖

You'll also like the upstairs display of astronauts' underwear and gear, including John Glenn's space suit. Imagine eating their in-flight food, such as freeze-dried beef hash and freeze-dried vegetables!

Take time out for the puppet theater. And test your knowledge of the universe in the game gallery. In the museum's planetarium, you can study the solar system.

There's a movie theater, too. But this isn't just any theater. It's 5 stories high and 7 stories wide and shows amazing films about flight.

Can you name the planets in our solar system? Their names have been scrambled to give you some hints.

CRUMEYR _____

NSEVU _____

HEART _____

RAMS _____

RIPEJTU _____

RUNSTA _____

SUNUAR _____

PEENUTN _____

TOULP _____

(Answers on page 146)

ARTS AND INDUSTRIES BUILDING

Would you like to see a steam locomotive or turn-of-the-century printing presses? You can if you visit the Arts and Industries Building.

You missed the 1876 Centennial Exposition in Philadelphia, celebrating America's hundredth birthday. But in 1976, the exposition was re-created in the Arts and Industries Building for the Bicentennial. There's lots to see from the original fair, which featured the latest technological advances of 1876. It's like a trip back in time where you can view carriages, musical instruments, furnishings, old machinery, and much more. Outside, there's a carousel that operates year round (weather permitting) and a Victorian garden to wander through.

Did you know?

President Garfield held his inaugural ball here in 1881.

Year round, you'll be entertained by singers, mimes, dancers, and puppets in the Discovery Theater. The Museum Shop is a must to visit. It looks like an old country store, where you can buy candles, jams, jellies, needlepoint, and other handmade goodies.

HIRSHHORN MUSEUM AND SCULPTURE GARDEN

There's a very unusual outdoor sculpture plaza that's part of the Hirshhorn Museum. You'll find it behind the building on Jefferson Drive. Let's see how skilled you are in a sculpture hunt.

In the garden and on the outdoor plaza of the museum, see if you can find the following: a "geometric mouse" made of black aluminum; a statue of a singing girl, called *Song*; and a figure titled *Man Pushing the Door*. How many legs does he have? Can you find the "three red lines"? (Hint: they're 37 feet

Did you know?

A sculpture can be made out of many materials, including wood, stone, metal, clay, glass, wax, plaster, and plastic.

78

TRAVEL DIARY

My favorite sculpture is _____. It's made out

of _____ and looks like _____.

I like it because _____

❖ ❖ ❖

tall and sway in the wind.) Locating Kenneth Snelson's *Needle Tower* is hardly like finding a "needle in a haystack." The tower is as high as a 6-story building. Few people know that if you look under the "needle," you'll see a star. See it? Be sure to find *The Burghers of Calais* by French sculptor Auguste Rodin. (Burghers, pronounced like *hamburgers* without the *ham*, are townspeople, and Calais is a seaport in France.) Note the eyes of the men.

Most people think of Henri Matisse and Pablo Picasso as painters, but they have sculptures here, too. Can you find their names? Inside the building, there's more sculpture, plus modern art of every type. See how different Deborah Butterfield's scrap-metal horse in the lobby is from the many horse statues you've seen on Washington's streets.

MUSEUM OF AFRICAN ART

A unique collection of art of a far different kind is only steps away in the Museum of African Art. It is the only museum in the U.S. devoted to black Africa, and has artwork from 900 African cultures. Notice the nearly life-size beaded carving of a German soldier who befriended an African king. There also are bronze portraits of Nigerian kings, traditional African costumes, musical instruments, and jewelry. Imagine wearing the 6-inch gold earrings worn by some African women!

Test yourself

Q: Can you guess what the opening in the stomach of the 3-foot-high *Power Figure* was used for?

A: To hold religious objects and medicine.

Did you know?

Because African tribes moved around a lot, they carried their valuables with them or wore them as jewelry. The size of a woman's gold earrings was a sign of wealth. The bigger the earrings, the richer she was.

NATIONAL GALLERY OF ART

Straight across the Mall on your right is another treasure house of artwork, the National Gallery of Art. Works here run from the Middle Ages (thirteenth century) to today. Here hangs the only Leonardo da Vinci painting in the Western Hemisphere. In addition to pieces by famous old masters like Rembrandt and Rubens, see works by French, Spanish, and American artists, including Winslow Homer and Georgia O'Keeffe.

Test yourself

Q: Rubens was a very famous artist but few people know his first name. What is it?

A: Peter.

CAN YOU NAME THESE MONUMENTS?

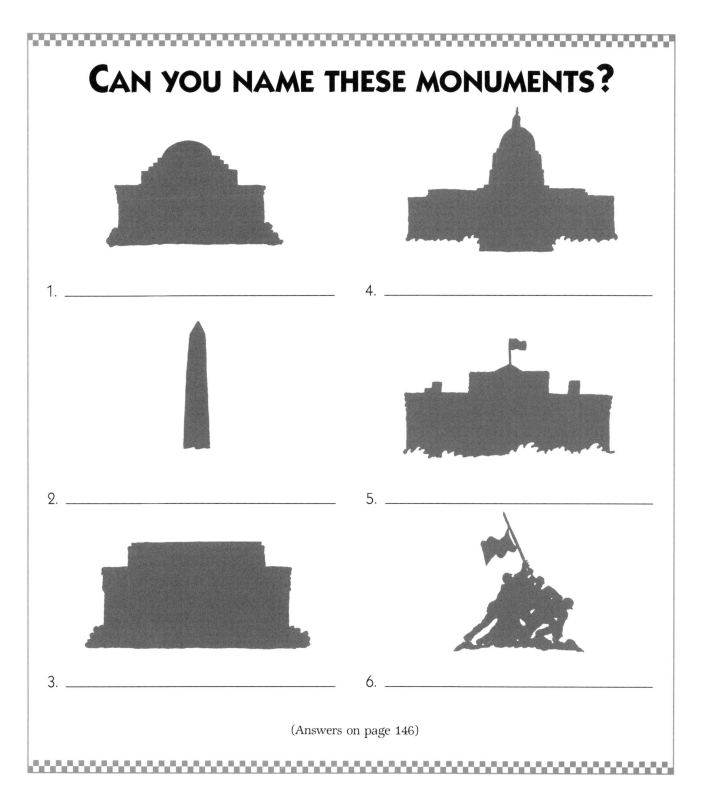

1. _____

2. _____

3. _____

4. _____

5. _____

6. _____

(Answers on page 146)

T·R·A·V·E·L D·I·A·R·Y

_____ art. The best

I like _____ .

art I have seen is _____ .

I like it because _____

If I made some art for a museum it would be _____

_____

(Draw a plan of your masterpiece here.)

❖ ❖ ❖

Did you know?

The prices of famous paintings have become so high that even museums don't have enough money to buy some of them. One painting of irises by Vincent van Gogh fetched nearly $54 million in 1987.

Take part in the Great Picture Hunt. Ask at the information desk in the gallery's west wing and you'll receive a map and guide, just like you would in a treasure hunt. It will send you off in search of a handful of the gallery's most exciting works. These include Rubens's painting of Daniel in the lion's den; Titian's portrait of a 12-year-old boy, painted 450 years ago; Auguste Renoir's picture of a girl with a watering can; and Winslow Homer's painting of a fisherman with 3 boys. When you find a picture, see if you can answer the questions about it and locate the items the guide mentions.

If you have lots of time, there is a similar hunt for paintings with monsters in them and paintings of parties. For those of you visiting on a Saturday morning during the school year, the gallery has a special family program in which you view a film and are then taken to related paintings. For instance, if you see a film on castles, you'll be led to paintings that show what life in a castle was like.

Before leaving, walk over to the east wing of the gallery, which has lots of large, fun sculptures and wall hangings. There's so much to see.

T·R·A·V·E·L D·I·A·R·Y

Of all the museums I visited on this trip, I like the _____
_____ best. It's full of
_____. The best thing about it is
_____. If I could have my own museum, I
would call it _____, and inside I would have
a collection of _____.

The Smithsonian Institution is so big, I didn't get to see it
all. I went to _____ of the buildings. On my next visit here,
I will spend most of my time in the _____
_____. My very favorite thing I saw in the
Smithsonian was the _____. I liked it because
_____.

❖ ❖ ❖

What Else Is There?

So far, we've stayed pretty much in the heart of Washington, D.C. But there is a lot more to this city. There are beautiful gardens, canal boats to ride, games to play, and places so old it's like traveling back through time.

A TOWN WITHIN A CITY— GEORGETOWN

Georgetown is a charming village brimming with history. It was the first port on the Potomac River. Ships unloaded luxury goods and furniture from England in exchange for tobacco from the colonies, bringing London elegance to this small port city. Many of Georgetown's brick "row houses" are 1 to 2 centuries old. The oldest house in Washington (built in 1765) is on M Street, and looks very much like it did before the American Revolution. You can visit the **Old Stone House,** where people dressed in colonial garb demonstrate how some homemaking tasks, such as spinning and quilting, were done.

Did you know?

Georgetown was founded almost 50 years before Washington, D.C., was created.

■ ■ ■

Row houses are a string of narrow houses that share walls with the homes on either side. Therefore they only have windows in the front and back.

85

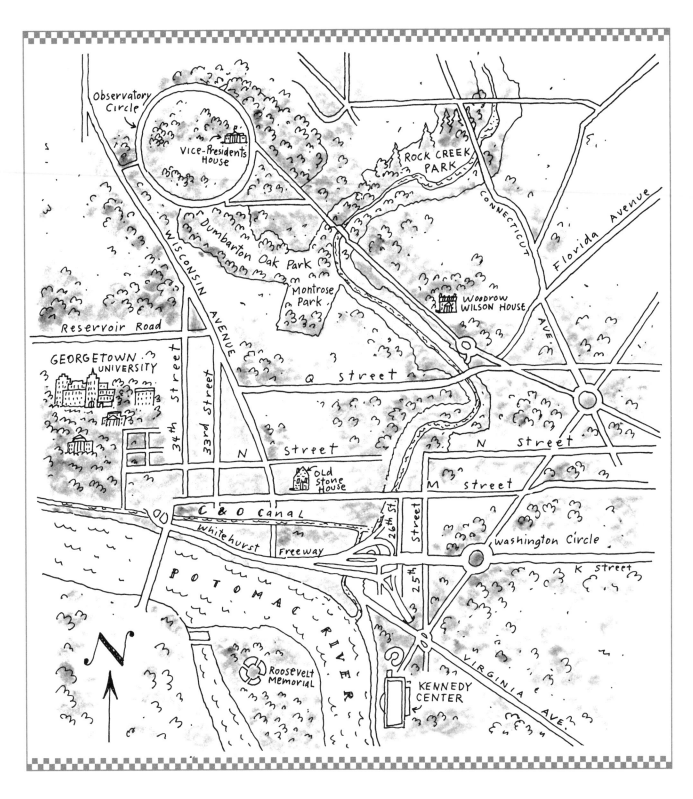

Did you know?

The Chesapeake and Ohio Canal was designed to link Washington, D.C., to Pittsburgh, Pennsylvania in the 1820s. It was only finished as far as Cumberland, Maryland. Railroads turned out to be faster.

■ ■ ■

A canal boat could carry as much as 120 tons of coal from the mountains of Maryland to the port of Georgetown.

■ ■ ■

A family lived aboard the canal boat and the children walked alongside the mules on the towpath to make sure the mules behaved.

■ ■ ■

During World War II a conference held at Dumbarton Oaks laid the groundwork for the creation of the United Nations.

■ ■ ■

At 2803 P Street you'll see a fence made of Civil War musket barrels.

One block south of the Old Stone House runs the **C & O Canal,** where mule-drawn boats were once used to haul cargo. The boats still operate in summertime, but carry tourists instead of cargo. Today people often jog and bike along the mule "towpath." Try to visit on a Sunday afternoon around 2:00 P.M. when there are free band concerts.

At the north end of Georgetown is **Dumbarton Oaks,** a beautiful old estate of terraces, fountains, and gardens perfect for romping. It is open to the public every afternoon.

Next to Dumbarton Oaks is **Oak Hill Cemetery,** with many old tombstones. Look over by the chapel for the grave of John Howard Paine, author of the song "Home, Sweet Home."

Walking or riding along the cobblestone streets of Georgetown is fun. Take a look at houses where famous people once lived: John F. Kennedy stayed at 3307 N Street before he was president; Jackie Kennedy lived at 3017 N Street after her husband was killed; Robert Todd Lincoln, the only surviving son of Abe Lincoln, lived at 3014 N Street. Elizabeth Taylor lived at 3252 S Street when she was married to Senator John Warner.

The only former president's house in Washington open to the public is the **Woodrow Wilson House** at 2340 S Street, just east of Georgetown. After he left the White House, Wilson lived here until his death in 1924.

The house is just as it was then. You can see objects from the White House and elaborate gifts of state from around the world. The house is also a living textbook of "modern" American life in the 1920's, from sound recordings to silent films to flapper dresses still hanging in the closets. Also fascinating are the elevator built in 1915 and the kitchen, which has a coal stove and oven, zinc sinks, and one of the first electric refrigerators.

88

Did you know?

Francis Scott Key, author of "The Star-Spangled Banner," used to live at 3512 M Street in Georgetown. A freeway is there now, but a bridge that connects Georgetown to Virginia bears his name.

■ ■ ■

Woodrow Wilson was president during World War I.

T·R·A·V·E·L D·I·A·R·Y

There are many old, big, and beautiful houses in Georgetown.

The best I saw was the _____.

It had _____

If I could live in a house like one of these, it would have _____

rooms and look like _____.

❖ ❖ ❖

SOMETHING OLD, SOMETHING NEW

The next stop looks old but is actually quite new. Here are a few clues to its identity. Can you guess what it is?

President Woodrow Wilson and Helen Keller are buried here, but it is not a cemetery.

The foundation stone contains a rock from a field in Bethlehem and was laid by a U.S. president.

Martin Luther King, Jr., preached his last sermon here.

Did you know?

Worship services have been held in the Washington Cathedral daily since 1912.

■ ■ ■

The Washington Cathedral is the sixth largest cathedral in the world. The top of its tower is 676 feet above sea level and the highest point in Washington.

Did you know?

A flying buttress is a stone arch coming out from a wall to support it. There is no structural steel in the Washington Cathedral.

■ ■ ■

Gargoyles, which look like devilish creatures, are used as waterspouts. They carry water away from a building through a hole in their mouths.

You're right: it's a church. But not just any church. It's the **Washington Cathedral**, a "national" church that everyone is invited to attend. Creating a national church was a dream of George Washington, but work on the cathedral wasn't actually begun until 1907.

A lot of people come just to look at this modern version of a fourteenth-century Gothic cathedral. Like the ancient cathedrals, it has flying buttresses, gargoyles, and stained-glass windows. A reminder that the cathedral is new, however, is the piece of moon rock embedded in the stained-glass Space Window. See if you can find it. Then see if you can locate the Lincoln pennies in the floor.

Be sure to visit the Children's Chapel, where everything is built to a child's scale. But, for the most fun of all, go to the Educational Resource Room, where you'll get a hands-on "look" at the craftsmanship that goes into making cathedrals, such as stained-glass work and stone carving.

ESPECIALLY FOR KIDS

To discover what it was like for kids living in the eighteenth and nineteenth centuries, head for the **Daughters of the American Revolution (DAR) Museum.** Don't bother with the main part of the building. Go right to the New Hampshire Toy Attic on the third floor, which has games, toys, and children's furniture from the 1800s. You'll see small china figures about 3 inches long, rag dolls, tea sets, miniature cast-iron stoves, and board games very much like you play today.

Did you know?

Windsor chairs were very popular in the eighteenth century. They were made of wood, with a rounded back made of spindles.

Across the hall is the Discovery Room, for children ages 3 to 12 and their parents. This is full of mystery boxes and items from the eighteenth and nineteenth centuries that you can touch. Feel a Braille flag from the late eighteenth century, or flax from which clothing was made. Learn about the furniture your ancestors probably used, and sit in a Windsor chair. Before leaving, be sure to see the museum's life-size replicas of rooms with colonial furnishings. One room is made from the wood of a British battleship sunk during the revolutionary war.

Washington also has a museum just for toys. It's called the **Washington Dolls' House and Toy Museum.** All of the games, toys, and dolls are very old. Of special interest is the Victorian mansion with lots of tiny furnishings, including a crank wall phone that really works, a piano that plays, and miniature pets. But there are other unusual dollhouses, too: a 1903 New Jersey seaside hotel; a lavish Mexican home with a working elevator, an aviary with birds, and a furnished chapel; Noah's ark, with all the animals; 5 Baltimore row houses; and an old-fashioned Ohio schoolhouse with a bell you can ring.

Did you know?

Flora Gill Jacobs, who runs the Dolls' House and Toy Museum, is a well-known dollhouse expert and author on the subject. She can answer your questions and even help you start a collection.

T·R·A·V·E·L D·I·A·R·Y

The best old toys I've seen were _____.

If I could have something from one of the toy museums, I'd like the _____, because _____

_____

Of all my toys at home, my favorite is _____

because _____

❖ ❖ ❖

The Lionel train from the 1930s with signals and sound effects is sure to be a hit. If it's not running, ask a guide to operate it.

Don't get played out yet, though. There's lots more in store. At the **Capital Children's Museum** everything is hands-on. You can make Mexican hot chocolate, tortillas, and paper flowers. Lift weights you never thought you could with levers and pulleys in the Simple Machine Corner.

In the communications area, see telephones of the future. Send a message on a teletype, or by Morse code using a ship's blinkers, or by African drums. Print a page from Ben Franklin's printing press.

Did you know?

You can leave your shadow on a special wall at the Capital Children's Museum.

Explore the world of animation and learn how to use a storyboard using inks and paints. Do a good job and you can have fun putting on your own cartoon show.

Try out different occupations: give yourself a sight test, play with doctors' equipment, or try on a mail carrier's bag for size. There's a Metro bus to drive, a real fire pole to slide down, a maze to explore, and plenty of games and lessons on computers. You'll be encouraged to touch, feel, smell, taste, wear, and use all the exhibits.

You'll enter and leave the museum through a unique garden filled with people. Talk to them for as long as you like, but don't expect an answer. These silent watchers are sculptures made entirely from junk.

SCIENCE AND YOU

Perhaps your parents get *National Geographic* magazine. It takes readers on pictorial trips to the far corners of the globe and the galaxy. Now imagine walking into the pages of the magazine and you've just pictured **National Geographic Society Explorers Hall.** Here you can investigate the earth's deserts, jungles, mountains, oceans, and even outer space through various exhibits, photos, and films.

You'll hear the story of early man unfold as Lucy, a 2.5 million-year-old skeleton, talks to a robot professor. You'll wonder how Mexican Indians made the giant head of carved stone they left on the jungle floor more than 4 centuries before the birth of Christ. See a model of the diving saucer used by underwater explorer Jacques Cousteau, an egg of the 1,000-pound extinct elephant bird, a "Goliath Frog" of Africa (2 feet long!), and Henry, the museum's live macaw.

One of the most breathtaking exhibits is a giant revolving globe of the world that's 34 feet around the equator. It weighs 1,100 pounds. See if you can find your home state.

Did you know?

The diving saucer has taken men and cameras to depths of 1,000 feet to study the Mediterranean and Red Seas.

MILITARY SHIPS AND WEAPONS

The Pentagon, headquarters of the U.S. military, is located across the Potomac River in Virginia. It is the world's largest office building. Imagine 17.5 miles of hallways, 280 bathrooms, and 150 staircases in 1 building! Aside from the 5-sided structure itself, though, there is not a lot to see—except offices!

If you're excited by military things, far more interesting is a stop at the **Navy Yard** in southeast Washington. This used to be where weapons were made, but now it's a museum. You can aim the barrel of a World War II ship's gun, turn submarine periscopes, operate anti-aircraft weapons, and go aboard a destroyer. Climb into the mock-up of a space capsule and sit in a bathysphere—that's a deep-sea research vessel.

Did you know?

Cannons on board nineteenth-century frigates such as the *Constitution* weighed 3 tons and needed 9 to 14 men to load and shoot them.

WHAT'S WRONG WITH THIS PICTURE? There are 10 things in the Navy Yard Museum that shouldn't be here. Can you find them?

(Answers on page 146)

Be sure to go on the Scavenger Hunt, which sends you searching for various weapons and military gear. There are guns and ship models dating from revolutionary war times to today, including a ship model that used to be in President Kennedy's office.

Did you know?

Bonsai trees never get big because they are clipped constantly. The arboretum has one that is more than 360 years old but will only reach to about your knees.

. . .

Willow was the original source of aspirin. You can see it in the herb garden.

Did you know?

The Navy Yard's submarine, *Trieste*, went to the deepest part of the ocean to see if anything could live at 35,000 feet. Yes, there was sea life.

STOPPING TO SMELL THE ROSES

Where can you see 70,000 azaleas, a dye garden, and a tree more than 3 centuries old? Or shrubs that were given to America by Soviet leader Nikita Khrushchev in 1960? Or a tree that is extinct in the wild? Or a type of redwood tree that grew when dinosaurs walked the earth 25 to 40 million years ago?

If you guessed the **National Arboretum,** a 444-acre garden in northeast Washington, D.C., you were right. This amazing garden also has dwarf evergreen trees and miniature bonsai trees. Special gardens grow herbs from which medicines were made, herbs used for cooking, and herbs used to dye clothes.

There are 9.5 miles of roads to drive down and numerous footpaths to wander along. Don't miss the reflecting pool containing colorful Japanese koi that look like giant red goldfish. The most exciting time to visit is in the spring, when the azaleas, dogwoods, cherry blossoms, and wildflowers are in bloom.

Color in the flowers and trees and unscramble their names.
The pictures will give you hints.

GOODWOD   __ __ __ __ __ __ __

ALEASZA   __ __ __ __ __ __ __

MORECHOSRYSSBL __ __ __ __ __ __ __ __ __ __ __ __ __

CHORDSI   __ __ __ __ __ __

PRAYSUNFELTVS   __ __ __ __ __ __ ' __ - __ __ __ __ __

ROBENASIET   __ __ __ __ __ __ __ __ __

LATESILEWIR   __ __ __ __ __ __ __ __ __ __

(Answers on page 146)

If it's impossible to get to the arboretum, however, there's no excuse for not seeing the **Botanic Gardens** on the Mall at the foot of the Capitol. The highlight of this giant greenhouse is orchids—there are always about 200 on display. But there are plenty of other flowers, all in a lush, relaxing setting of waterfalls, pools, and fountains. See the vanilla tree, which gives us vanilla flavoring; the "chocolate" (cacao) tree, whose seed is used to make chocolate; and the coffee tree, which produces coffee beans. During the summer months you can see plants that eat insects, such as the Venus's-flytrap.

Did you know?

There are more than 30,000 kinds of orchids in the world. They grow on every continent except Antarctica.

■ ■ ■

One type of plant at the Botanic Gardens, called a *cycad*, has remained unchanged for 200 million years—since long before the dinosaur. That's why it is called a *living fossil*.

■ ■ ■

A type of water lily called a *lotus* was believed sacred by people in some countries.

For a garden of a different kind, try the **Kenilworth Aquatic Gardens** in northeast Washington, which has the largest group of water lilies and aquatic plants in the world. This floating garden has been described as a treasure hidden away from Washington's mainstream. See lotus blossoms as big as a human face and water lilies that are red, blue, pink, and purple. In August, one lily has leaves that reach 7 feet in diameter.

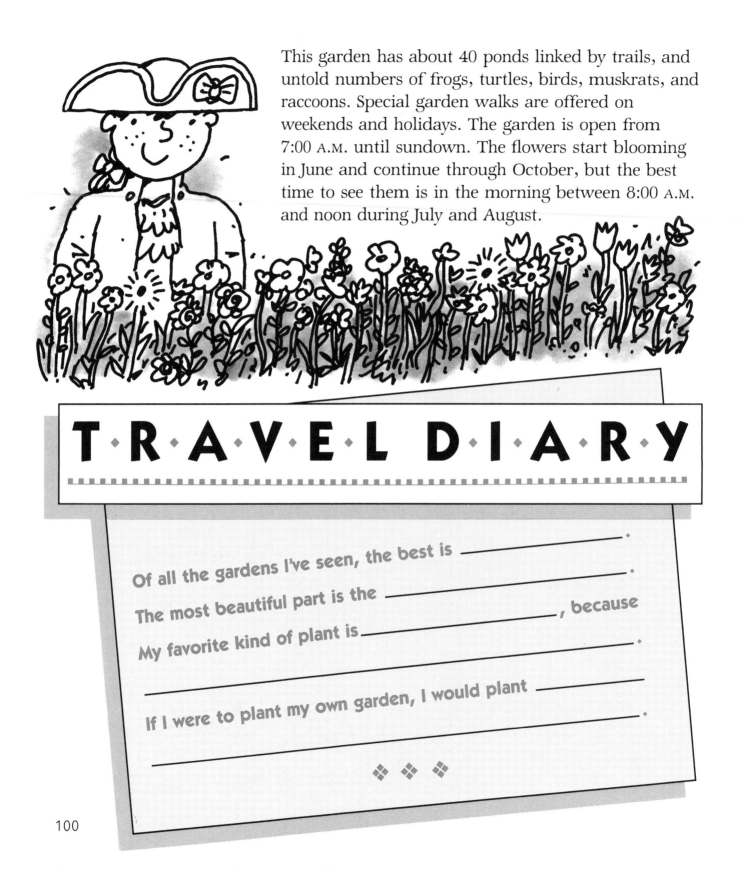

This garden has about 40 ponds linked by trails, and untold numbers of frogs, turtles, birds, muskrats, and raccoons. Special garden walks are offered on weekends and holidays. The garden is open from 7:00 A.M. until sundown. The flowers start blooming in June and continue through October, but the best time to see them is in the morning between 8:00 A.M. and noon during July and August.

T·R·A·V·E·L D·I·A·R·Y

Of all the gardens I've seen, the best is _____.

The most beautiful part is the _____.

My favorite kind of plant is _____, because

_____.

If I were to plant my own garden, I would plant _____.

❖ ❖ ❖

Where Are All the Animals?

Did you know?

Smokey the Bear may look brown, but he is really an American black bear.

THE NATIONAL ZOOLOGICAL PARK

Washington isn't just a city of historical figures, diplomats, and politicians. There are other famous residents—of the four-legged variety. For instance, you can see Kumari, the first elephant to be born in this zoo (December 1993), and the Komodo dragons, the first to breed in the western world.

These creatures and many others can be found at the National Zoo, located in Rock Creek Park. The best time to visit is in the early morning or in the late afternoon, because this is when the animals are most active.

Did you know?

A good time to visit the zoo is at feeding time.

Pandas: 11:00 A.M. and 3:00 P.M.
Most other animals: 9:00 to 10:00 A.M. and 2:00 to 3:00 P.M.

The zoo's food bill for its animals runs $750,000 a year.

101

Twenty-seven percent of the animals in the zoo are endangered species in the wild.

The giant pandas from China are among the most famous residents of the zoo. They are picky eaters, preferring bamboo—to the tune of 30 pounds a day each.

Many other zoo residents also come from foreign countries. There is a pygmy hippo from Liberia, a rhinoceros from India, an elephant from Africa, and monkeys from Brazil that look like lions. You will see these golden lion tamarins roaming free in the valley during the summer.

The first thing to do when you arrive at the zoo is to stop by the Education Building for a map and a list of special programs being offered that day. Here you can also get tickets for ZOOlab—available on a first-come basis—which features short films, zoology textbooks, and hands-on learning with things like hummingbird eggs. You can even look at specimens through a microscope. There are two other "labs": HERPlab, a center for the study of reptiles and amphibians (you can get tickets in the middle of the House of Reptiles); and BIRDlab, an educational program for the study of birds (no tickets needed). All 3 programs are fun and informative.

Make sure you visit the exhibit of unusual creatures that don't have backbones. They look like eerie characters from a Stephen Spielberg space film. And don't leave without stopping by the Ape House to watch the antics of the gorillas and orangutans, or by the House of Reptiles, Beaver Valley, and the walk-in bird cage where you can mingle with 68 different kinds of birds.

Did you know?

For many years, the zoo had a famous resident from outer space. He was Ham, the late chimp who made a space flight about a month before we put our first astronaut, Alan Shepard, into orbit in 1961.

103

T·R·A·V·E·L D·I·A·R·Y

My favorite animal is the _____ , because

_____ . It looks like

_____ . Some of the most unusual animals

_____ . They were

I saw were _____ .

unusual because _____

If I could take an animal home with me, I'd choose a

_____ , because _____ . If I could be

any kind of animal I wanted, I would be a _____

and my name would be _____ .

❖ ❖ ❖

THE NATIONAL AQUARIUM

Just as there are 3,000 animals at the zoo, there are more than 1,000 underwater creatures waiting to entertain you at the National Aquarium. It's located in the basement of the Department of Commerce Building.

Did you know?

Zombies are people who have been put in a trancelike state in order to obey the commands of others. Sometimes they are called *the walking dead*.

One interesting species you'll see here is the puffer fish. Can you find one? Did you know that medicine men in Haiti used the poison found in these fish to create zombies?

Go over to the Touch Tank and pick up a horseshoe crab. Did you know that these crabs have 4 eyes and blue blood, and that they're more closely related to a spider than a crab?

A creature from outer space got into the zoo and zapped the animals with its vanishing gun. Fortunately, the gun didn't work correctly and parts of the animals can still be seen. Help Gulliver restore the animals by adding the correct letters to the names below. Hint: They have lined up in alphabetical order.

```
AN _ EL _ PE        _ IGHTINGALE
BA _ OON            O _ L
CHE _ TAH          P _ _ DA
DE _ R             _ UAIL
E _ EPH _ NT       RA _ _ OON
_ OX               SQ _ IR _ EL
G _ RAF _ E        TI _ E _
_ YEN _            _ NICO _ N
I _ UANA           VAM _ IRE  BA _
JAG _ AR           WO _ F
KAN _ A _ OO       X
LE _ PARD          YA _
M _ USE            ZE _ RA
```

(Answers on page 146)

Perhaps you'd like to watch piranhas at dinnertime. They're the famous flesh-eating fish that swim in schools of thousands and can reduce a man to a skeleton within minutes. You're in luck. There are feed shows on Tuesdays, Thursdays, and Sundays at 2:00 P.M. Sorry, they don't get live people—only frozen fish and squid.

Did you know?

Sharks grow a nonstop supply of teeth.

▪ ▪ ▪

Sharks can sniff out a single drop of blood in 1 million drops of water.

Other attractions are a 7,000-gallon tank full of sharks, 3 sea turtles named Sea-cil, Mar-shell, and Myrtle, and 3 alligators named Gitcha, Getcha, and Gotcha. There is also an array of sea creatures with strange talents: fish that swim upside down, and even—are you ready for a shock?—electric fish.

UNUSUAL FARMS

There are lots of other fun places to see animals in and around Washington, D.C. There are many farms, but not the kind of farms you're used to. One farm operates just like it did in colonial times. Another lets you help bring in the harvest, milk a cow, or cook a meal. Still another has exotic animals you can pet and ride. How about telling friends back home you rode a camel or a gigantic turtle?

The **Claude Moore Farm at Turkey Run** in McLean, Virginia, is the farm of a lower-income family, run just as it was in 1771. A family in costume goes about the daily chores using only eighteenth-century tools and planting only eighteenth-century crops. They may even invite you to help with the chores!

At the **National Colonial Farm** in Accokeek, Maryland, you'll see a middle-class tobacco plantation from 1750. Don't be surprised to see the cattle, sheep, lambs, ponies, and chickens running free. In those days, crops were fenced in for protection, while the animals roamed at will.

Did you know?

The Claude Moore farm has colonial cattle, whose horns haven't been cut off, and pigs that aren't pink but black and white (and smaller and hairier than those common nowadays).

■ ■ ■

There was no indoor plumbing in the 1800s, and so in the bedrooms you'll see chamber pots, which served as temporary toilets.

Believe it or not, you can see a stuffed 2-headed calf in the veterinarian's office of the **Carroll County Farm Museum** in Westminster, Maryland. This mid-to-late 1800s farm has a farmhouse, blacksmith and tinsmith shops, nature trails, and a collection of horse-drawn vehicles to be explored. Baby goats, lambs, pigs, turkeys, chickens, and rabbits can be seen in the barns.

You can help to gather eggs, milk a cow, or grind feed for the horses at **Oxon Hill Farm** in Oxon Hill, Maryland, a working farm from the early 1900s. On most weekends there's even a hayride.

Children on a colonial farm learned farming skills from the time they were toddlers by working alongside their parents in the fields.

■ ■ ■

Storytelling was a primary form of entertainment, much as television is today.

But if you want to ride a camel or a pony, touch the stripes of a zebra, or watch an egg hatch, the place to go is **Pet Farm Park** in Vienna, Virginia. Here you're invited to feed the animals and cuddle the rabbits, chicks, calves, goats, and pigs in the Petting Barn. Tractor hayrides will give you a close-up look at some of the larger creatures—antelope, elk, buffalo, ostrich, eland, and bighorn sheep.

There's even a miniature **Old MacDonald's Farm** in the heart of Maryland's Wheaton Regional Park. Also in the park is the **Brookside Nature Center**, with trails, wildlife feed areas, and picnic groves.

You'll find **Rock Creek Nature Center** located in the midst of 1,750 acres of hardwood forest, the last remaining forest within Washington, D.C.'s city limits. The exhibit hall has an owl, snakes, toads, turtles, and a working beehive. Test your senses on the Touch Wall, where you stick your hand in a hole and guess what you're feeling. Nearby, you can catch the center's planetarium show.

A relaxing stop along the George Washington Memorial Parkway—heading south toward Alexandria, Virginia—is **Roaches Run Waterfowl Sanctuary**. This is a year-round haven for water birds of all types—mallard, pintail, and bufflehead ducks, finches, wrens, and American egrets.

Are We Going to Eat?

LUNCHING IN A MUSEUM

By now you're probably ready to eat. Some of Washington's most interesting restaurants are in museums and government buildings.

Pick out your lunch from any number of dishes on a giant revolving carousel at the Museum of American History or the Air and Space Museum.

Munch on a sandwich among exotic works of art at the outdoor plaza cafe of the Hirshhorn Museum and Sculpture Garden.

If riding an underground moving sidewalk builds up your appetite, go to the lower floor of the east wing of the National Gallery of Art. The sidewalk will drop you off at a cafe next to a gigantic indoor waterfall.

One of the most popular museum eateries is *Patent Pending*, a cafeteria in a courtyard linking the National Portrait Gallery with the National Museum of American Art. Sit among fountains and sculptures as you eat food that is both tasty and inexpensive.

But maybe you'd like to rub elbows with politicians and their staffs. If so, head to the *House of Representatives Restaurant* or the *Capitol Coffee Shop* on the House side of the Capitol. Or, order a grilled cheese sandwich and a hot fudge sundae in the *Refectory Restaurant* on the Senate side.

There are other government buildings with restaurants open to the public. Try the grill line for hamburgers and french fries in the Library of Congress James Madison Memorial Building. In the Supreme Court's cafeteria, you could end up sitting next to a judge! They eat there, too.

Did you know?

Bean soup has been served at the House of Representatives Restaurant since 1904, when Speaker of the House Joseph Cannon became outraged one day when he couldn't get it. He ordered that bean soup be placed on the menu every day. And so it has been.

DOWN BY THE WATERFRONT

What more pleasant way to eat than on a boat trip up the Potomac passing Washington's major monuments? A 3-hour dinner cruise on Washington Boat Lines' *Spirit of Washington* embarks from Pier 4 at Sixth and Water Streets, SW.

Did you know?

At noontime, the Washington Boat Lines serves a luncheon buffet on an hour-long cruise. And on Friday and Saturday nights, there's a moonlight cruise with munchies.

You say you want to keep your feet on solid ground, but still enjoy a river view? *Phillips Flagship* at 900 Water Street or *Hogate's Seafood Restaurant* (its rum buns are famous) at 9th and Maine Avenue in southwest Washington are good choices. Walk along Maine Avenue and you're apt to see oyster fishermen coming in with their catches, ships unloading cargo, tugboats, windjammers, and maybe even Washington's fireboat, *The Firefighter*.

The place with the best view in town is the glitzy *Potomac Restaurant* at the foot of Georgetown. Its windows overlooking the river are 2 stories high, and it has 21 huge crystal chandeliers and a lit jeweled ceiling with 800,000 glass gems. It is probably the fanciest restaurant you'll ever see.

Did you know?

Because most of the land that borders the river belongs to the government, there are few restaurants along the Potomac. But there's something almost as good. Weather permitting, you can always opt for a table alongside the C & O Canal at the *Fish Market Restaurant* in Georgetown.

T·R·A·V·E·L D·I·A·R·Y

While in Washington, D.C., I want to eat _____

_____. My favorite kind of food is

_____. Of all the food I've tasted

_____ the best.

here, so far I like _____

The _____ museum had the neatest-looking

cafeteria. Some of the fun places I ate were:

_____, where I had _____.

_____, where I had _____.

_____, where I had _____

_____

❖ ❖ ❖

FOOD FROM AROUND THE WORLD

How is your spirit of adventure? Because Washington attracts people from all over the world, its restaurants give you a chance to try food you would have a hard time finding in most parts of the country. So be brave—it may be a long time before you get another chance.

Where on the map are these places found?

Ethiopia	Japan	Vietnam
France	Italy	Germany
India	China	Spain

(Answers on page 147)

Following are some of the foods you can try. See if you can locate these countries on the map above.

Ethiopia—Not only is the food of this African nation different from U.S. fare, but you don't have to watch your table manners. It's the custom to eat with your fingers. Food is served on metal trays with a stack of pancakelike bread. Tear off a piece of the bread and

Did you know?

If you order Ethiopian food, it will seem like a feast. But remember, many people in Ethiopia are starving.

Can you match the kind of food with the country that it comes from?

sushi	India
chop suey	Japan
baklava	Italy
chapatis	Vietnam
spaghetti	China
spring roll	Greece

(Answers on page 147)

(Answers on page 147)

Did you know?

The countries of what is called the *Middle East* stretch from Afghanistan to Egypt.

use it to scoop up your meal. At the *Red Sea*, 2463 18th Street, NW, you and your family can get a sampler that includes a spicy chicken dish, lamb, beef strips, and a choice of 4 vegetables, such as spiced cabbage and yellow split peas. You'll hear Ethiopian music and people speaking the native language.

France—Be daring and sample the speciality of the house at *Chez Grand Mere*, 3057 N Street, NW, where the chef makes the best bouillabaisse this side of the Atlantic. Or, if you chicken out on the fish stew, visit *Monique Cafe et Brassiere*, 2500 Calvert Street, NW, where you can sink your teeth into sautéed crabcakes á la Maryland. One bite and you'll exclaim, "Boy, are these good!"

India—Believe it or not, more people eat Indian food than eat American apple pie and pot roast. That's because India has the second largest population in the world—3 times more than the U.S. The food of India should not be confused with American Indian fare. It is entirely different. Most people think of it as hot, spicy curry sauce on rice. But a lot of Indian food is mild. Most of it, however, is hard to pronounce. For instance, would you guess that *murgh zabunnisa* is a chicken dish, or that *chapatis* is grilled Indian bread? Probably not. To try this unusual food, go to the *Taj Mahal Restaurant,* 1327 Connecticut Avenue, NW. It's a good idea to ask your waiter for help in selecting your meal.

Japan—Have you ever eaten raw eel or shark or seaweed-wrapped rice? Well, here's your chance. A form of Japanese cooking (or *noncooking*, since the fish is served raw) called *sushi* has become very popular in the U.S. A sushi meal consists of thin strips of different kinds of fish folded around cakes of cold rice. The names of items are usually in Japanese, but most restaurants offer English descriptions. *Japan Inn,* at 1715 Wisconsin Avenue, NW is one that does.

Italy—If you don't want sushi but have a craving for spaghetti, homemade pizzas, and rotisserie chicken, try *Filomena Ristorante,* 1063 Wisconsin Avenue, NW. White-clad "pasta mamas" stuff ravioli while you wait.

Did you know?

Saigon, once the capital city of South Vietnam, is now known as Ho Chi Minh City.

Vietnam—Since the end of the Vietnam War, when many Vietnamese refugees came to America, the food of this Southeast Asian country has become quite popular. Chicken, beef, and fish dishes served with rice are typical. Your food may be eaten with chopsticks, but don't be embarrassed to ask for a fork. Try *Miss Saigon*, 1847 Columbia Road, NW, and tickle your taste buds.

Germany—You'll find breakfast, lunch, and dinner served at *Cafe Mozart*, 1331 H Street, NW, where you might order a veal cutlet (schnitzel), or beef pot roast (sauerbraten), or delicious German sausage. There's live music almost every night. You'll also find gourmet items at the cafe's delicatessen counter.

GOOD OLD AMERICAN FARE

Had enough exotic food? Want to get back to the basics of hot dogs, hamburgers, and pizza? You won't be disappointed in Washington, D.C. There are lots of fast-food chains—*Arby's, Burger King, Domino's Pizza, Gino's, McDonald's, Shakey's,* and *Wendy's,* to name a few.

Can I Have That?

On every vacation you want to buy gifts and souvenirs. No other city has the unusual items that can be found in Washington, D.C. For instance, you can wow your hometown friends by serving astronaut freeze-dried ice cream, or a chocolate milkshake just like pilots Dick Rutan and Jeana Yeager drank on their nonstop round-the-world 1987 *Voyager* flight. How about showing your classmates colonial currency or money that has been untouched by human hands? Or teach them a ball-and-cup game played by colonial children. Or let them feel your genuine shark's tooth.

All these souvenirs and many more can be had at little cost in the shops of Washington's many museums. These places specialize in items that are affordable, popular, and often impossible to find anywhere else.

YOUR OWN MUSEUM COLLECTION

The National Air and Space Museum, for instance, offers astronaut ice cream in a variety of flavors, as well as *Voyager* milkshakes and space games.

The Bureau of Engraving and Printing will sell you its brand-new money or, for a lower price, bags of shredded bills.

The National Aquarium not only has sharks' teeth, but whole sharks' jaws, as well as dried sea horses, starfish, and rubber "jump" frogs to add to your collection.

Did you know?

Two-dollar bills have not been printed since 1976 because they aren't very popular. But they are still around. You can buy them at the Bureau of Engraving's gift shop.

At the National Colonial Farm you can get colonial-style toys, such as the wooden ball-and-cup toss, tops, and tin whistles.

The Museum of American History will make you a personalized "dog tag" just like U.S. soldiers wear.

At the National Archives Building, pick up copies of our nation's Declaration of Independence, Constitution, and Bill of Rights. Or buy scarves imprinted with the signatures of all the presidents or all the signers of the Declaration of Independence.

You can get a whole packet of fake colonial or revolutionary wartime currency and a quill pen at the Jefferson Memorial gift shop.

Or, you can buy paper dolls in period clothes—from the Civil War to the 1980s—at the Ford Museum. Its Washington, D.C., coloring book also makes a nice gift for a friend at home because you can talk about your trip as he or she colors in the pictures.

If fossils or gemstones are more your style, stock up at the Museum of Natural History, where fake fossils, colorful necklaces, and bracelets are both pretty and affordable.

T·R·A·V·E·L D·I·A·R·Y

The best store I've ever been to was _____

The best thing they had was _____

I bought a _____ at the _____

The weirdest store I've seen in Washington, D.C., is _____

_____. They sell _____

_____

❖ ❖ ❖

For an extra special gift, how about a flag that has flown over the Capitol? They're available in both 3-by-5-foot and 5-by-8-foot sizes. The flags, however, must be ordered in advance through your senator or representative. Allow 4 to 6 weeks for delivery.

SHOPPING MALLS, STALLS, AND STORES

Museum shopping is fun and easy because you're already there. But Washington also has plenty of malls and shopping areas that are worth a visit.

One fun place to shop is the **Old Post Office**. This 1899 building was recently converted into a treasure chest of about 60 shops, crafts outlets, and international eateries called the **Pavilion**. You'll recognize the building at 1100 Pennsylvania Avenue by its 315-foot clock tower. Inside, ride the glass elevator to the tower's top. Afterward, browse among the shops. There's music and entertainment all day long on weekends. The third Saturday of every month is Children's Day, with lots of activities.

Did you know?

The Pavilion tower has 10 large bells just like those in England's Westminster Abbey. You can hear them on Thursday evenings between 6:30 P.M. and 9:30 P.M. when the bellringers practice.

Another popular mall—with some very unusual stores—in the heart of downtown at Pennsylvania Avenue and F Street is the **Shops at National Place.** Above its 3 levels of shopping and fast-food outlets rises the National Press Building, where journalists from countries all over the world, such as China and the Soviet Union, have their offices. There is probably even a reporter or two from your hometown.

When touring Georgetown with your parents, ask them to take you for a stroll through **Georgetown Park.** It's not a park but a shopping mall, one of the prettiest you'll ever see, nestled alongside the canal and featuring a marble fountain and glass skylight.

Shopping is a popular pastime in Georgetown. And there's no lack of trendy and upscale shops on Wisconsin Avenue and M Street. But beware: except for street vendors hawking jewelry and clothes, this is not a bargainer's paradise.

If huge malls are more to your liking, the Washington area has some of the biggest. Don't miss **Union Station** at 40 Massachusetts Ave., NE. This working train station houses 125 stores, restaurants, and a 9-screen cinema complex.

At this mall you're sure to find kites that fly, dolls that cry, and lots, lots more. You can even buy your Amtrack ticket here in case you wish to travel home by train.

You'll find more shopping malls outside the Washington area, but you'll have to go by car, bus, or taxi. **Tyson's Corner Mall** in McLean, Virginia, with more than 200 shops, is one of the busiest intersections in the U.S. If you're looking for bargains, computer terminals in the mall will provide you with the latest information on merchandise that's on sale.

On the Maryland side of Washington, you'll like the **White Flint Mall.** It has more than 110 stores, including *Lord & Taylor, Bloomingdale's,* and *I. Magnin.*

There are even underground malls that you can reach by subway. One is at the Pentagon, and another at Crystal City, across from Washington National Airport in Virginia.

Don't shop till you drop, however. Plan to take a shopping break in any one of the many food courts you'll find in the various malls. You might even decide to treat yourself to a refreshing ice cream cone until you feel ready to shop once more.

Are We Having Fun Yet?

Are you ready for a different kind of fun? How about renting a boat for an hour and pedaling around the Jefferson Memorial in the Tidal Basin, or flying a kite on the Mall? Or, better yet, heading to one of several amusement parks just a few miles from the White House? Most of them are only open during the summer, however, so check ahead of time.

DRAW A PICTURE OF SOMETHING FUN FROM YOUR TRIP.

GLEN ECHO PARK CAROUSEL

You don't have to go far to find a carousel. There's one right on the Mall, outside the Arts and Industries Building. But, for an unusual treat, head to Glen Echo Park, a few miles northwest of the city. On Wednesday mornings and weekend afternoons during the summer, ride its special carousel—one of only

Did you know?

The Glen Echo Park Carousel was installed in 1921 by the famous Dentzel Carousel Company of Philadelphia. It has horses, lions, tigers, giraffes, rabbits, and cats—each hand-carved by specialists. How many animals are there? Fifty-two.

▪ ▪ ▪

Many carousels have been taken apart and sold, piece by piece, to collectors. Glen Echo's was saved when citizens raised $80,000 to buy it.

Test yourself

Q: There is a lead, or "king," horse. Can you find it?

A: It's the largest one in the outside circle.

▪ ▪ ▪

Q: The outside horses are called *standers*. Can you guess why?

A: They each have at least 3 feet on the ground.

about 300 hand-carved wooden carousels still in existence. Child actors in the park's weekend Adventure Theater bring to life fables and fairy tales year-round. You can also see puppet shows, visit artists' studios in yurts (copies of ancient Chinese houses), or take a crafts workshop.

KINGS DOMINION

For an extra-big dose of entertainment, drive to Kings Dominion, the largest amusement park north of Florida. It's on the road to Richmond, Virginia, about 75 miles south of Washington. It has 1300 acres of fun and games. One of its rides, the Shockwave, is the East Coast's only stand-up roller coaster. Before the ride is over, you'll be turned sideways and upside down. Jump in a rubber raft and ply the White Water Canyon, matching wits with its riptides and rapids. Shoot down a water slide on a speeding sled that drops 3 stories in 3 seconds. (You don't need your bathing suit, because you land on dry ground.) Drive miniature antique cars. See the dolphin show or sing along with the Smurfs. And don't miss the 180-degree theater designed to make you feel like you're in the middle of chase scenes with dune buggies and speedboats.

Did you know?

The longest, highest, fastest roller coaster in the world is called the *Beast.* It is at the Kings Island amusement park in Kings Mills, Ohio—a sister park to Kings Dominion. The Beast is 1.4 miles long, 141 feet high, and can reach speeds of 72 mph.

Gulliver is lost in an amusement park. Help him find his way to the cotton candy.

Cotton Candy

FINISH

START

(Answer on page 147)

Did you know?

Adventure World's roller coaster was built in 1917 for Paragon Park in Boston. It was called the *Giant*. It has now been restored by the original maker.

ADVENTURE WORLD

If you're really feeling wild and crazy, the best place to be is Adventure World in Largo, Maryland. It has a roller coaster nicknamed the *Wild One* that was voted sixth best in the world in 1986 by a group of roller coaster lovers. For more thrills and excitement, don't miss the *Mind Eraser* and the *Python*, two high-speed looping coasters complete with rollovers, dives, sidewinders, and double spins. Escape to an island adventure the Swiss Family Robinson would have envied. There are shows, lots more dizzying rides, and a playground designed for the twenty-first century, with plenty of activities for both kids and parents.

Did you know?

Adventure World's wave pool may be one of the world's largest swimming pools. It holds 1 million gallons of water and 2000 people can swim at once!

T·R·A·V·E·L D·I·A·R·Y

Amusement parks are meant for kids. My favorite ride is the
_____.
_____, because _____
_____ amusement park.
It is in the _____, because
The ride I don't like is _____. When I went
_____,
on the _____ at _____
I got _____. There are lots of
good things to eat at amusement parks, too. I ate _____
_____
when I was at _____. Mmm . . . it was good.

❖ ❖ ❖

Is That All?

Well, isn't Washington, D.C., a great place to visit? There's so much to see and do—touring museums, government buildings, zoos, and farms. And there are great places outside of Washington, D.C., to visit, too—like Mount Vernon, Monticello, Jamestown, Williamsburg, and Baltimore—so many there's not enough room to tell you about them all.

For more ideas on what to do in Washington, D.C., call or write the Washington Convention and Visitors Association. For places of interest outside the Washington, D.C., area, call or write the Maryland Office of Tourist Development, or the Virginia Division of Tourism. (Telephone numbers and addresses can be found in the appendix.) Don't forget to ask about special programs for kids. Many organizations will send you information if you contact them directly.

Make full use of the addresses and telephone numbers in the appendix even before you leave for your trip. Some attractions mentioned in this book charge for admission, though many others are free. The more you plan ahead, the more you'll enjoy your trip.

T·R·A·V·E·L D·I·A·R·Y

I've seen a lot in Washington, D.C. Some places I went to that are not in this book are _____. My favorite thing to do in Washington is _____. If I come back, I will visit _____, but I won't visit _____, because _____.

I liked _____ the best, because _____.

When I get home, the first thing I will tell my friends is _____. The best day of the trip was _____, because _____. My favorite souvenir is _____. I got it at _____. The next trip I take, I want to go to _____ with _____.

❖ ❖ ❖

To reserve a place on special tours of the White House, Capitol, and other government agencies, call your representative or senator at his or her local office well in advance of your visit. They should also be able to send you brochures of places in Washington, D.C., that you might find interesting.

Once you're in Washington, pick up some of the free publications that list various events tourists may enjoy. The *Washington Post* is also a wonderful source of information, particularly on Fridays when the newspaper's "Weekend" section is included.

Remember, once you're in Washington, D.C., it's a very good idea to call ahead to double-check on the events you plan to attend. And above all, have fun.

C·A·L·E·N·D·A·R

JANUARY

Opening of Congress
Inauguration and festivities (every 4 years)
Martin Luther King Birthday Celebration (202) 619-7222

FEBRUARY

Chinese New Year Parade (202) 724-4091
Black History Month at Smithsonian (202) 357-2700
Black History Month Salute to Black Artists (202) 332-2879

MARCH

Smithsonian Kite Festival (202) 357-3030
Cherry Blossom Festival (202) 646-0366
St. Patrick's Day Parade (301) 424-2200

JULY

Independence Day Celebration on the Mall (202) 619-7222
Festival of American Folklife at Smithsonian (202) 357-2700
Caribbean Summer in the Park (202) 249-1028
DC World Jazz Festival (202) 783-0360

AUGUST

Georgia Avenue Day Parade (202) 723-5166
Friday Evening Parades at Marine Barracks (202) 433-6600
Civil War Reenactment (703) 361-7181
Maryland Renaissance Festival (703) 361-7181

SEPTEMBER

International Children's Festival (703) 941-1527
Labor Day Concert (202) 785-8100
Adams-Morgan Day (202) 332-3292/ (202) 832-4274
Rock Creek Park Day (202) 426-6832
Washington Cathedral Open House (202) 537-6200
Friday Evening Parades at Marine Barracks (202) 433-6060
DC Blues Festival (202) 828-3028

For more details, check with Washington, D.C., Convention and Visitors Association, 1212 New York Ave., NW, Washington, D.C. 20005. (202) 789-7037.

APRIL

White House Easter Egg Roll (Easter weekend) (202) 456-2200

Duke Ellington Birthday Celebration (202) 331-9404

Thomas Jefferson Birthday Celebration (202) 426-6700

White House Spring Garden Tour (202) 456-2200

Smithsonian's Washington Craft Show (202) 357-2700

MAY

Greek Spring Festival (202) 829-2910

Friday Evening Parades at Marine Barracks (202) 433-6060

Memorial Day Services (202) 789-6060

Worldfest Festival (202) 724-5430

JUNE

Children's Festival (202) 619-7222

Unifest (202) 724-5430

Sunday Afternoon Polo (202) 426-2700

Wianki Festival of the Wreaths (202) 789-7000

Friday Evening Parades at Marine Barracks (202) 433-6060

OCTOBER

Opening Ceremony of the Supreme Court (first Monday)

U.S. Navy Band Birthday Concert (202) 433-6090

White House Fall Garden Tour (202) 426-6700/(202) 472-3669

Halloween Program (703) 838-4343

Marine Corps Marathon (703) 640-2225

Annual Showcase Black Theater (202) 529-5763

Sunday Afternoon Polo (202) 426-6700

NOVEMBER

Washington's Review of the Troops (703) 549-0205

Armistice Day Celebration (202) 673-4034

Veterans Day Celebration (202) 475-0843

DECEMBER

Festival of Music and Lights (301) 587-0144

Carol Singing (703) 255-1900

Lighting of the National Christmas Tree (202) 628-3400

Christmas Pageant of Peace (202) 628-3400

Traditional Smithsonian Holiday Celebration (202) 357-2700

African American Market Place & Festival (202) 737-1670

Christmas Pageant (202) 537-6200

New Year's Eve Celebration (202) 289-4224

A·P·P·E·N·D·I·X

ADVENTURE WORLD   (301) 249-1500. 13710 Central Ave., Largo, MD. 10:30 A.M.–9:00 P.M. daily, Memorial Day–Labor Day. (May be open weekends in Sept.; call for information.)

ARLINGTON NATIONAL CEMETERY   (703) 692-0931. Arlington, VA. 8:00 A.M.–5:00 P.M. daily, Oct.–Mar.; 8:00 A.M.–7:00 P.M. daily, Apr.–Sept.

ARMED FORCES MEDICAL MUSEUM   (202) 576-2341/ (202) 576-2418 (recording). Walter Reed Army Medical Center, 6825 16th St., NW. 9:30 A.M.–5:00 P.M. Mon.–Fri.; 11:30 A.M.–5:00 P.M. Sat., Sun., & holidays. Closed Thanksgiving, Christmas Eve & Day, New Year's Eve & Day.

ARTS AND INDUSTRIES BUILDING   (202) 357-2700. 900 Jefferson Dr., SW. 10:00 A.M.–5:30 P.M. daily. Closed Christmas.

BOTANIC GARDENS   (202) 225-8333. Maryland Ave. & 1st St., SW. 9:00 A.M.–5:00 P.M. daily, Sept.–May; 9:00 A.M.– 9:00 P.M. daily, June–Aug. Closed Christmas.

BROOKSIDE NATURE CENTER   (301) 946-9071. Wheaton Regional Park, 1400 Glenallan Ave., Wheaton, MD. 9:00 A.M.– 5:00 P.M. Tues.–Sat.; 1:00 P.M.–5:00 P.M. Sun. Closed Mon. & holidays.

BUREAU OF ENGRAVING AND PRINTING   (202) 447-9709. Corner of 14th & C Sts., SW. 9:00 A.M.– 2:00 P.M. Mon.–Fri. Closed weekends, national holidays, & week between Christmas and New Year's Day.

CAPITAL CHILDREN'S MUSEUM   (202) 543-8600. 800 3rd St., NW. 10:00 A.M.–5:00 P.M. daily. Closed national holidays.

CAPITOL   (202) 224-3121/(202) 225-6827 (tours). East end of the Mall. 9:00 A.M.–10:00 P.M. Easter & Labor Day. Closed Thanksgiving, Christmas, & New Year's Day.

CARROLL COUNTY FARM MUSEUM   (410) 876-2667. 500 Center St., Westminster, MD. Noon–5:00 P.M. Sat. & Sun. Also open 10:00 A.M.–4:00 P.M. Tues.–Fri. in July & Aug.

CHESAPEAKE AND OHIO CANAL   (202) 472-4376. Between 30th & Thomas Jefferson Sts., Georgetown/ (301) 739-4200. Office of the Superintendent, C & O Canal National Historical Park, P.O. Box 4, Sharpsburg, MD/ (301) 299-3613. National Parks Service, Great Falls Tavern.

CLAUDE MOORE COLONIAL FARM AT TURKEY RUN (703) 442-7557. 6310 Old Georgetown Pike, McLean, VA. 10:00 A.M.–4:30 P.M. Wed.–Sun., Apr.–Dec. Closed Jan.–Mar., Mon., Tues., Thanksgiving, Christmas, & rainy days.

DAUGHTERS OF THE AMERICAN REVOLUTION (DAR) MUSEUM   (202) 879-3239. 1776 D St., NW. 9:00 A.M.– 4:00 P.M. Mon.–Fri., 1:00 P.M.–5:00 P.M. Sun. Tours: 10:00 A.M.– 2:15 P.M. Mon.–Fri.; 1:00 P.M.–5:00 P.M. Sun. Closed Sat.

DUMBARTON OAKS   (202) 338-8278. 1703 32nd St., NW. 2:00 P.M.–6:00 P.M. daily, Apr.–Oct., 2:00 P.M.–5:00 P.M. daily, Nov.–Mar. Closed national holidays.

◆   ◆   ◆   ◆   ◆

FEDERAL BUREAU OF INVESTIGATION (202) 324-2892. E St. (between Ninth & Tenth Sts.) 8:45 A.M.–4:15 P.M. Mon.–Fri. Closed weekends & all national holidays.

FORD'S THEATRE AND LINCOLN MUSEUM (202) 638-2368. 511 10th St., NW. 9:00 A.M.–5:00 P.M. daily. Closed Christmas & during matinee performances.

GEORGETOWN INFORMATION CENTER (202) 472-4376. 1055 Thomas Jefferson St., NW.

GLEN ECHO PARK (301) 492-6282. MacArthur Blvd. & Goldsboro Rd., Bethesda, MD. Open all year for classes. Check on summer weekend events. Carousel: Noon–6:00 P.M. Sat. & Sun.; 10:00 A.M.–2:00 P.M. Wed. Closed Oct.–Apr.

HARBORPLACE Corner of Pratt & Light Sts., on Baltimore Harbor. 10:00 A.M.–10:00 P.M. daily. Restaurants close at 2:00 A.M.

HIRSHHORN MUSEUM AND SCULPTURE GARDEN (202) 357-2700. 7th St. & Independence Ave., SW. 10:00 A.M.–5:30 P.M. daily. Closed Christmas.

IWO JIMA STATUE Route 50, near Arlington National Cemetery. Open daily, 24 hours.

JEFFERSON MEMORIAL (202) 426-6841. Tidal Basin (south bank). 8:00 A.M.–midnight daily. Closed Christmas.

JOHN F. KENNEDY CENTER FOR THE PERFORMING ARTS (202) 467-4600/1-800-444-1324. 2700 F St., NW. 10:00 A.M.–1:00 P.M. daily. Free guided tours.

KENILWORTH AQUATIC GARDENS (202) 426-6905. Kenilworth Ave. & Douglas St., NE. 7:00 A.M.–sundown daily. Closed Christmas. Tours weekends & holidays. (Flowers bloom mid-June-Oct.)

KINGS DOMINION (804) 876-5000. Route 30, Doswell, VA. 9:30 A.M.–8:00 P.M. daily, Memorial Day–Labor Day; 9:30 A.M.–10:00 P.M. daily, July & Aug. Open weekends only in late Mar., Apr., May, Sept., & early Oct.

KOREAN WAR MEMORIAL (202) 426-6700. Constitution Ave. between Henry Bacon St. & 21st St., NW. Open daily.

LIBRARY OF CONGRESS (202) 707-2905. 10 1st St., SE. 8:30 A.M.–9:30 P.M. Mon.–Fri.; 8:30 A.M.–6:00 P.M. Sat. Closed Sun. & holidays. Tours: 9:00 A.M.–4:00 P.M. Mon.–Fri.

LINCOLN MEMORIAL (202) 426-6841. West Potomat Park at 23rd St., NW. Open daily, 24 hours. Closed Christmas. (Tours available upon request.) Free.

LURAY CAVERNS (703) 743-6551. Luray, VA. 9:00 A.M.–4:00 P.M. daily. (Extended seasonal hours vary.)

MARYLAND OFFICE OF TOURIST DEVELOPMENT (410) 333-6611. 217 East Redwood St., Baltimore, MD 21202.

MATTAPONI INDIAN RESERVATION (804) 769-2194. Route 30, West Point, VA. 10:00 A.M.–5:00 P.M. Mon.–Sat.; 2:00 P.M.–5:00 P.M. Sun. Open Thanksgiving, Christmas, & Easter by appointment only.

METROBUS (202) 962-1122. Call for route information. Full information center at Metro Center Station, 12th & F Sts., NW. Buses run 5:30 A.M.–midnight Mon.–Fri.; 8:00 A.M.–midnight Sat. & Sun.

MUSEUM OF AFRICAN ART (202) 357-2700. 9th St. & Independence Ave., SW. 10:00 A.M.–5:30 P.M. daily. (extended spring/summer hours vary yearly.) Closed Christmas.

MUSEUM OF AMERICAN HISTORY (202) 357-2700. 14th St. & Constitution Ave., NW. 10:00 A.M.–5:30 P.M. daily. (Extended spring/summer hours vary yearly.) Closed Christmas.

MUSEUM OF NATURAL HISTORY (202) 357-1650. 10th St. & Constitution Ave., NW. 10:00 A.M.–5:30 P.M. daily. (Extended spring/summer hours vary yearly.) Closed Christmas.

NATIONAL AIR AND SPACE MUSEUM (202) 357-1400. 6th St. & Independence Ave., SW. 10:00 A.M.–5:30 P.M. daily. (Extended spring/summer hours vary yearly.) Closed Christmas.

NATIONAL AQUARIUM (202) 482-2826/(202) 482-2825. Department of Commerce Building (lower level), 14th St. & Constitution Ave., NW. 9:00 A.M.–5:00 P.M. daily. Closed Christmas.

NATIONAL ARBORETUM (202) 544-8733. 3501 New York Ave., NE. Open daily.

NATIONAL ARCHIVES (202) 501-5200 7th St. & Pennsylvania Ave., NW. 10:00 A.M.–5:30 P.M. daily, Sept.–Mar.; 10:00 A.M.–9:00 P.M. daily, Apr.–Aug. Closed Christmas.

NATIONAL COLONIAL FARM (703) 283-2113. 3400 Bryan Point Rd. Accokeek, MD. 10:00 A.M.–5:00 P.M. Tues.–Sun. Closed Mon., Thanksgiving, Christmas, & New Year's Day.

NATIONAL PORTRAIT GALLERY   (202) 357-2700. 8th & F Sts., NW. 10:00 A.M.–5:00 P.M. Mon.–Sat.; noon–9:00 P.M. Sun. (Extended spring/summer hours vary yearly.)

NATIONAL GEOGRAPHIC SOCIETY EXPLORERS HALL (202) 857-7455. 1600 M St., NW. 9:00 A.M.–5:00 P.M. Mon.–Sat. Closed Sun. & holidays. Closed Christmas.

NATIONAL PARK SERVICE   (202) 426-6841. Call to reserve space in the "Under the Lincoln" tour. Or write in advance to Mall Operations, 900 Ohio Dr., Washington, DC 20242. No tours during summer.

NATIONAL ZOOLOGICAL PARK   (202) 673-4800. 3000 block of Connecticut Ave., NW. 8:00 A.M.–6:00 P.M. daily, mid-Sept.–Apr.; 8:00 A.M.–8:00 P.M. daily, May–mid-Sept. Buildings: 9:00 A.M.–4:30 P.M. daily, mid-Sept.–Apr.; 9:00 A.M.–6:00 P.M. daily, May–mid-Sept. Closed Christmas.

NAVY YARD AND NAVY MUSEUM   (202) 433-4882. Washington Navy Yard, 901 M St., SE. 9:00 A.M.–4:00 P.M. Mon.–Fri., Sept.–May; 9:00 A.M.–5:00 P.M. Mon.–Fri., June–Aug.; 10:00 A.M.–5:00 P.M. Sat. & Sun. Closed Thanksgiving, Christmas Eve & Day, & New Year's Day.

OLD MACDONALD'S FARM   (301) 622-0056/ (301) 949-6615 (carousel)/(301) 949-6615 (train). Wheaton Regional Park, Wheaton, MD. 9:00 A.M.–sunset daily. Closed Thanksgiving, Christmas, & New Year's Day.

OLD STONE HOUSE   (202) 426-6851. 3051 M St., NW. 9:30 A.M.–5:00 P.M. Wed.–Sun. Closed Mon., Tues., Thanksgiving, Christmas, & New Year's Day.

OXON HILL FARM   (301) 839-1176. 6411 Oxon Hill Rd., Oxon Hill, MD. 8:30 A.M.–5:00 P.M. daily. Closed Thanksgiving, Christmas, & New Year's Day.

PAMUNKEY INDIAN RESERVATION   (804) 843-4792. King William, VA. 9:00 A.M.–4:00 P.M. Mon.–Sat.; 1:00 P.M.–5:00 P.M. Sun. Closed major holidays.

PAVILION AT THE OLD POST OFFICE   (202) 289-4224. 1100 Pennsylvania Ave., NW. Tower: 10:00 A.M.–6:00 P.M. daily, Oct.–Mar.; 8:00 A.M.–11:30 P.M. daily, Apr.–Sept. Pavilion: 9:00 A.M.–10:00 P.M. daily.

PENTAGON   (703) 695-1776. Washington Blvd., bordering Arlington National Cemetery. 9:30 A.M.–3:30 P.M. Mon.–Fri. Closed weekends & holidays. Free tours available.

PET FARM PARK   (301) 759-3636. 1226 Hunter Mill Rd., Vienna, VA. 10:00 A.M.–5:00 P.M. daily, June–Oct.; 10:00 A.M.–3:00 P.M. Mon.–Fri., late Mar.–June; 10:00 A.M.–5:00 P.M. Sat. & Sun., late Mar.–June.

PETERSEN HOUSE   (202) 426-6830. 516 10th St., NW. 9:00 A.M.–5:00 P.M. daily. Closed Christmas.

ROACHES RUN WATERFOWL SANCTUARY (202) 285-2600. Off George Washington Memorial Pkwy., south of 14th St. Bridge. Open all year. Call for hours.

ROCK CREEK NATURE CENTER   (202) 426-6829. 5200 Glover Rd., NW. 9:00 A.M.–5:00 P.M. Wed.–Sun. Planetarium shows: 1:00 P.M. & 4:00 P.M. Sat. & Sun., (for children 4 and older); also 3:45 P.M. Wed. Closed Mon., Tues., & holidays.

SMITHSONIAN INSTITUTION BUILDING   (The Castle) (202) 357-2700. 1000 Jefferson Dr., SW. 10:00 A.M.–5:30 P.M. daily. Closed Christmas & New Year's Day.

SUPREME COURT   (202) 479-3030. 1st & Maryland Ave., NE. When in session, the Court meets Mon.–Wed. 10:00 A.M.–3:00 P.M. When not in session, free lectures 9:30 A.M.–3:30 P.M. each half-hour. Closed all federal holidays. Call or write your congressional representative for tour two months in advance.

TOMB OF THE UNKNOWN SOLDIER   Route 50, near Arlington National Cemetery. Open daily, 24 hours.

TOURMOBILE SIGHTSEEING   (202) 554-5100. 1000 Ohio Dr., SW. Narrated shuttle tour. Stops at White House, Washington Monument, Smithsonian museums, Arlington National Cemetery.

VIETNAM VETERANS MEMORIAL   (202) 426-6700. Constitution Ave. between Henry Bacon Dr. & 21st St., NW. Open daily, 24 hours.

VIRGINIA DIVISION OF TOURISM   (804) 786-2051/ 1-800-932-5827. 901 East Byrd St., Richmond, VA 23219.

WASHINGTON BOAT LINES   (202) 537-6200. Pier 4 at 6th & Water Sts., SW. Open late Mar.–first week in Nov. Call for departure times and costs.

WASHINGTON CATHEDRAL   (202) 537-6200.
Mount St. Alban at Massachusetts & Wisconsin Aves., NW.
10:00 A.M.–4:30 P.M. Mon.–Sat.; 8:00 A.M.–5:30 P.M. Sun.
Tours: 10:00 A.M.–3:15 P.M. Mon.–Sat. (except during
services); 12:30 P.M. & 2:00 P.M. Sun. Call the Department of
Educational Programs at (202) 537-2930) for information
about special programs for children. Closed Christmas &
New Year's Day.

**WASHINGTON CONVENTION AND VISITORS
ASSOCIATION**   (202) 789-7037. 1212 New York Ave., NW,
Suite 600, Washington, DC 20005.

WASHINGTON DOLLS' HOUSE AND TOY MUSEUM
(202) 244-0024. 5326 44th St., NW. 10:00 A.M.–5:00 P.M.
Tues.–Sat.; noon–5:00 P.M. Sun. Closed Mon., Thanksgiving,
Christmas, & New Year's Day.

WASHINGTON MONUMENT   (202) 426-6841. On the
Mall at 15th St., NW. 9:00 A.M.–5:00 P.M. daily, Sept.–Mar.;
9:00 A.M.–midnight daily, Apr.–Aug. Closed Christmas.

WASHINGTON TOURIST INFORMATION CENTER
(202) 789-7000. 14th St. & Pennsylvania Ave., NW (in Great Hall
of the Department of Commerce building). 9:00 A.M.–5:00 P.M.
daily, Closed Sun. Oct.–Mar.
Dial-an-Event: (202) 737-8866
Dial-a-Park (National Parks Services): 426-6975
Dial-a-Museum (Smithsonian Institution): (202) 357-2020

WHITE HOUSE   (202) 456-2322/(202) 456-2200 (special
events)/(202) 456-7041 (tours). 10:00 A.M.–noon, Tues.–Sat.
Closed Sun., Mon., Christmas, New Year's Day, & for
presidential functions.

WOODROW WILSON HOUSE   (202) 387-4062. 2340 S St.,
NW. 10:00 A.M.–4:00 P.M. Tues.–Sun. Closed Mon. & major
holidays.

C·A·R G·A·M·E·S

Long car rides don't have to be boring or drive you crazy. Playing games will make the time fly. You don't have to sit still and get sore, stiff, and restless either. Stretch out and move your tired muscles with some easy car exercises. They'll keep you from wishing you could roll down the window and scream or kick open the door and jump out.

Games are for fun, so laugh it up and play the ride away.

Things to take along on any long ride:

- something hard and flat to write on—like a tray, board, or large hardcover book
- coloring pens, pencils, or crayons
- pad of paper or notebook
- deck of cards
- books to read

WORD GAMES:

Think of as many names as you can for each letter of the alphabet. *D*: Debbie, Doug, Diane, Denise, Dan, and so on.

Look for each letter of the alphabet on car license plates as they pass (you can skip the hard-to-find letters *Q* and *Z*).

Make words out of the letters you see on car license plates. For example: 125 BHV, say *beehive*.

Packing for your trip: Name things you can put in your suitcase starting with the letter *A*, then *B*, then *C*, and so on. For example: Apple, Baseball, Cat, Dictionary (they don't really *have* to be things you need on your trip).

COUNTING GAMES:

Watch car license plates and count the numbers, starting with zero. See who can reach 9 first. Or keep counting to 20—it takes longer.

Find the most: Pick something to count and see who can find the most. You can pick things like green cars, stop signs, license plates from Washington, D.C., people driving with hats on, kids in cars, and so on.

GUESSING GAMES:

20 Questions: Think of something for the others to guess. They ask you questions to try to figure out what it is. You can only answer "yes" or "no." If no one guesses in 20 questions, you win. Or you can just let them keep asking questions until someone figures it out.

Pictionary (like dictionary, but with pictures): Like 20 Questions, someone is "it" and thinks of something that everyone else tries to guess. You draw pictures for them to give them clues and hints—but you can't draw what the answer is. You could pick the name of your school. Then, for clues, you could draw your classroom, desk, schoolbook, lunch box, or teacher—or anything else you might think of. Draw pictures until someone guesses what it is you're thinking of.

DRAWING:

One person draws a mark, line, shape, letter, or number, and someone else has to make a picture out of it.

STORIES:

One person starts to make up a story. The next person has to add the next line or sentence to the story; then on to the next person. Everyone in the car takes a turn making up the story line-by-line. It can turn out to be a pretty funny story. You might even end up on the moon with a _____ .

Make up a travel friend: This is your chance to say anything you want about your trip. You pretend that you have an invisible friend taking the trip with you. Only you can see and hear your friend, so you have to tell everyone else what your friend is saying. Does he or she like your car? Where does she want to go tomorrow? What does he like to eat? You can say ANYTHING. Make up a story about where your friend is from, what his or her family is like—or whatever you want.

CARDS:

Bring along a deck of cards and play your favorite games. Or, if there's room, you can turn a hat over and try to toss the cards into it. You have to throw them as if they were tiny Frisbees.

MOVEMENT GAMES:

Charades: Someone acts out a kind of animal (or anything else) using only face and hands. Everyone else has to guess what she or he is.

Simon Says: Someone is Simon. Everyone else has to do whatever Simon says—but only when Simon says, "Simon says. . . ." If Simon doesn't say this and you do what he or she says, you goof. Like this: "Simon says, 'Touch your nose with your right hand.' " (Simon touches his nose. Everyone else does, too.) Simon gives lots of directions, then he sneaks in an order without saying "Simon says" but does it anyway. If anyone follows, he or she goofs.

Statue: Everyone playing this game freezes into a statue. See who can stay that way the longest without moving.

Making Faces: Someone is "it." He or she makes a face—sad, goofy, happy, sleepy, cranky—and the other person has to imitate the face. This simple game is really a crack-up.

EXERCISES:

You'll be amazed at how much exercise you can get while riding in a car. You can't swim, run, or throw a ball, but you can work out by stretching your muscles. Make up your own stretches, or do

page 113

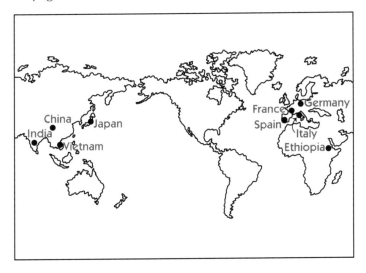

page 128

page 114

sushi — Japan
chop suey — China
baklava — Greece
chapatis — India
spaghetti — Italy
spring roll — Vietnam

PHOTO CREDITS

■■■■■■■■■■■■■

Page	Courtesy of
11	Washington, D.C., Chamber of Commerce
14	NASA
19	Roloc Color Slides
24	National Archives, Washington, D.C.
27	Library of Congress, from *Harper's Weekly*, May 20, 1882
28	Washington, D.C., Chamber of Commerce
29	Washington, D.C., Chamber of Commerce
33	Washington, D.C., Chamber of Commerce
35	Roloc Color Slides
36	Roloc Color Slides
39	Washington, D.C., Chamber of Commerce
42	Roloc Color Slides
47	Bureau of Engraving and Printing
52	U.S. Department of Justice, Federal Bureau of Investigation
53	National Archives, Washington, D.C. (*Washington at Dorchester Heights* by Gilbert Stuart)
54	Roloc Color Slides
55	New York Historical Society, New York City (portrait)
55	Washington, D.C., Chamber of Commerce (memorial)
56	Library of Congress; Photo by Gardner, 1865
57	National Park Service, Ford's Theatre NHS (*Death of President Lincoln* by Alexander H. Ritchie)

Page	Courtesy of
58	Washington, D.C., Chamber of Commerce (memorial)
58	National Portrait Gallery, Smithsonian Institution, Washington, D.C. Artist: William F. Draper, 1966 (portrait)
59	Roloc Color Slides
61	Virginia Division of Tourism; Arlington, The Custis-Lee Mansion, Arlington, VA
62	Washington, D.C., Chamber of Commerce
63	Smithsonian Institution, Photo #78-9318
66	Smithsonian Institution, Photo #77-3520 (African Bush Elephant)
66	Smithsonian Institution, Photo #43493 (triceratops)
70	Smithsonian Institution, Photo #84-6808-5A
72	Division of Graphic Arts, National Museum of American History, Smithsonian Institution
74	National Air and Space Museum, Smithsonian Institution, Photo #85-17676-22 (1903 flyer)
74	National Air and Space Museum, Smithsonian Institution, Photo #78-18444-9 (Friendship 7)
77	Debra and Robert Bretzfelder/ PhotoEdit
80	National Museum of African Art, Smithsonian Institution, Photo by Jeffrey Ploskonka

Page	Courtesy of
83	East Building Interior Courtyard, National Gallery of Art, Washington, D.C.
85	Roloc Color Slides
87	C & O Canal, NHP/Donna J. Donaldson
90	Alex Martin (window)
90	Washington National Cathedral (gargoyle)
91	DAR Museum
93	Washington Dolls' House & Toy Museum
95	Roloc Color Slides
101	National Zoological Park
102	Ilene Berg, National Zoological Park, Smithsonian Institution
107	Carroll County Farm Museum, Westminster, Maryland. Photographed by Paul Breeding.
120	Debra and Robert Bretzfelder/ PhotoEdit
121	Debra and Robert Bretzfelder/ PhotoEdit (National Press Building)
121	Georgetown Park (Georgetown Park Mall)
125	Maryland Office of Tourist Development
126	National Park Service, Glen Echo Park
127	King's Dominion
129	Wild World

Photo research by PhotoEdit, Tarzana, CA